To Don Green
Spirit!

D1231072

F#11 Feb. 6, 2001)

THE
URGENT
REVOLUTION

By Dwight Whitsett

Dwight Whitsett

**Additional Books available
from:**

Dwight Whitsett <u>dwibren@mindspring.com</u>
4025 Fairmont
Abilene, TX 79605
Web: <u>www.whitticisms.com</u>

The Urgent Revolution

By Dwight Whitsett

Published by:
SOMERSET ROAD PRESS
381 CASA LINDA PLAZA, #229
DALLAS, TX 75218

All rights reserved. No part of this book may be reproduced or transmitted in any form or by any means, electronic or mechanical, including photocopying, recording or by any information storage and retrieval system without written permission from the author, except for the inclusion of brief quotations in a review.

Copyright © 1997 by Dwight Whitsett

Scripture qoutations, unless otherwise noted, are from the Holy Bible: New International Version. © 1973, 1978, 1984 by the International Bible Society. Used by permission of Zondervan Bible Publishers. Those marked NASB are scripture taken from the NEW AMERICAN STANDARD BIBLE ®, © Copyright The Lockman Foundation 1960, 1962, 1963, 1968, 1971, 1972, 1973, 1975, 1977. Used by permission.

ISBN: 0-9658634-0-9

SOME COMMENTS FROM OTHERS ABOUT *THE URGENT REVOLUTION*

Cline Paden: A mere perusal of the Table of Contents will excite the mind of the most discriminating reader. **A BRILLIANT ANALYSIS OF THE PROBLEMS FACING THE CHURCH TODAY.** This, together with achievable solutions to those problems, gives this book a prominent rating on a list of books to read and re-read. It is easy to read, and each sentence so masterfully crafted that the thought of laying it aside will not occur.

Jim Woodroof: "Christ~entered and practical and holistic. One of the best I've read in a long time. **ON THE SUBJECT...I DON'T KNOW OF A BETTER ONE.** Few books have impacted me as yours did. I'm a better man for having read it. It 'fanned my gift into a flame.' . ..this book must be published and distributed widely."

Richard Rogers: Only occasionally do I read something broad enough to include all believers and still unique enough to address the real problems in one brotherhood. *The Urgent Revolution* is such a book. **THIS BOOK NEEDS TO BE READ BY ALL WHO HONOR CHRIST AND HIS CHURCH.** His analogy is correct, his contribution is significant, his diagnosis is accurate and his solution is biblical.

Leonard M. Gray: "The only thing I found negative about this outstanding book is that it will not be read by everyone who needs to read it.. and that is everyone! It is **SOLID, CHALLENGING, DISTURBING, NEEDED!** The chapter on "The Dreaming" is not only worth the price of the book.. .it is also rich in "what-if's" and "just imagine's" as to make us a little "giddy." But what if we should see that dream realized! Thank you, Dwight, for this book.

Truitt Adair: "You expressed so succinctly, the almost inexpressible frustrations of so many thoughtful Christians as they contemplate the way we "do church" and the way we relate to a lost world. **AT ONCE HUMOROUS, CHALLENGING, EDIFYING AND VERY READABLE.** Although some will likely disagree with a few conclusions, anyone who loves our brotherhood and lost people will be challenged to rethink how they do, or perhaps how they do *not* do evangelism."

Avon Malone: "Dwight Whitsett confronts the reader with the needed but painful challenge to change by embracing the intense passion of early Christians in reaching the lost. He forces Christians to make a reality check on the actual health of the church. **REMARKABLE CANDOR PLUS ENGAGING WITH A *"MUST - READ"* FOR CONCERNED CHRISTIANS.** While some might have reservations about specific suggestions for attacking the anemia and apathy thwarting Christ's commission, we can all concur with his diagnosis and treatment."

Sandy Bell: "It reads easily...anecdotal references smooth its way. The urgency is fully justified -- by scripture, by circumstances. **PASSION COUPLED SO BEAUTIFULLY WITH THOUGHTFUL BIBLICAL PERSPECTIVE...FINAL CHAPTER IS AN ABSOLUTE BLOCKBUSTER.** The message is both a warning and a certain trumpet sound to move -- sometimes back, sometimes forward, but very sure of our authority... destiny... mandate."

William D. Tate: *The Urgent Revolution* is a biblical compendium of thought-provoking ideas for the modern-day Christian. Filled with earthy examples, unshrouded language, and inspirational challenges..." **A 'CALL TO ARMS' TO REPEL SOCIAL FORCES AND AGGRESSIVELY DISSEMINATE THE GOSPEL OF CHRIST.** It is a fresh new approach to Christian methodology that can only be undermined by the ancient problem of traditionalism."

Robert McKinnon: "You can feel Dwight Whitsett's passion for both the situation and the hardball decisions that must be made to change the course of local churches and the way they think about their mission. **THE URGENT REVOLUTION IS A BOLD TREATISE TO THE CHURCH AT THE RIGHT TIME.** It is admirable to take a stand while saying it with such color of word, illustration and smoothness. This work is easy reading..."

ACKNOWLEDGMENTS

Over the years, many men and women representing a wide spectrum in my fellowship have exerted a profound influence upon me. **Joe Banks, Paul Cantrell, Jack Paul, Avon Malone, Abe Lincoln, Tex Williams, Richard Rogers, Johnny Ramsey, Ed Wharton,** and **Cline Paden** have, through the years, challenged and shaped my thinking. They gave me a passionate love for preaching, teaching and writing about the word of God and its application to our lives.

Added to this list must be my grandmother **Sudie Hale**, my aunt **Margaret Hale Alexander**, and especially my mother **Luvenia Hale Whitsett**. The constant encouragement and instruction of these women has impacted my life beyond calculation.

Former co-workers **Edward McGeachy** and **Mel Ashby** have provided brotherly love, encouragement, and a listening ear. I love you guys!

Patty Crowley, editor with Sweet Publishing Company greatly encouraged me in the early stages of writing this book. I seriously doubt that this book would exist if not for her early generous appraisal. Also, special thanks to **John Hunter,** editor with College Press, for being on my side and urging me to keep on praying and not give up.

Great gratitude is due my precious and talented family! My beloved **Brenda** performed the final edit. Her gift for finding weaknesses and suggesting improvements is beyond value to me. My daughter, **Amy Hopkins**, patiently designed and typeset this book in the midst of many demands. My Eldest son, **Tim Whitsett**, is responsible for the magnificent cover art.

Thanks to our lifeline, **Stan Poyner**. Without his support this book would still be a dream.

Others who have been very helpful and encouraging are **Merri Dennis, Sandy Bell, John Bell, Pat Jones, Bob McKinnon, Bill Tate, Roger Guess, Richard Minix, James Nix, Garry Sullivan** and so many more. Undying gratitude to you all!

To Brenda.
Encourager, Companion, Lover, Best Friend.
Ego Amo Te

TABLE OF CONTENTS

PREFACE

To be able to put that burr under your blanket, that pressurized head of steam, into print is both cathartic and therapeutic. Flimsy and disorganized thoughts assume an organized and tangible form. An ambiguous and cluttered discussion becomes solid and concise The message of this book burns within me and I must *say* it or be *consumed* by it. For many years the need to speak has been building up like a thunderhead. The updrafts of disappointment and frustration have drawn together in clouds of growing conviction. Now the lightning flashes and the downpour begs for release. I am aware that the ensuing storm may damage me in some eyes. To others, I will have rained a few inches too much (perhaps on their parade). I will annoy others who expected gully-washer and got a shower. Three decades of experience make the impossibility of pleasing everyone very clear.

My fellowship is the Church of Christ. This book will inevitably reflect my heritage much the same as a book by a Presbyterian or Methodist will reflect theirs. I have, however, been impressed that the challenges we face in Churches of Christ are the same, in principle, as those faced by other fellowships. It will be easy for the thoughtful reader to make application to his own situation in his own fellowship.

If God grants me my "three-score and ten," I am now about two-thirds through my race. What you will read is the product of that journey. It is the distilled essence of the experiences God has given me on the way.

The Urgent Revolution represents the way I feel now in these days surrounding the turn of the century. Two thousand years have come and gone since the Word became flesh and dwelt among us. Who knows what the years ahead may bring should we be spared to live them? Right now, I stand convicted of a message. Is it from God? Well, I didn't hear any voices or receive any visions. I have, however, definitely felt an *urgency* to put pen to paper. This book is the result of a lot of hard thinking about the church of our Savior. I am confident in the validity and effectiveness of the principles of this book. I believe they are *biblical,* derived from the life and teaching of Jesus and His apostles. The direction and focus of Jesus and the apostles must become ours. The inhabitants of our planet are enslaved, divided and condemned. *Why* and *How* must Jesus' disciples make the modifications necessary to bring his gospel redemption and reconciliation to them? The answer becomes a message of paramount importance; one of *transformation* so needful I dare to call it an *urgent revolution.*

Dwight Wallace Whitsett

1

THE CHURCH IN CHAINS

As Jesus' church we have confined ourselves in a jail of our own making. Combining ignorance and misconception, we waylaid the Way, and chained ourselves to cold, clammy walls with chains of division and enmity. Now the cause of Christ languishes in the dungeon of tradition and apostasy.

Here's the odd part: there are no locks! We are free to go! We remain in the damp darkness because we are unaware of our freedom. The lock is on our mind! To liberate the cause of Christ, we must liberate our thinking. The truth will set us free! If we change our thinking we can walk out into fresh air and sunshine.

The New Testament church needs no changes. Jesus built a masterpiece we dare not alter. The manifestations and direction of the church are a different matter. The church today suffers from generally poor health. The symptoms tell us the patient urgently needs examination, honest appraisal, and adjustment. We enter a new century schizophrenic, anemic, distracted and unfocused. Two thousand years of religious fermentation have brewed up something tragically unlike the church of the Bible. As an out-of-focus projection of Jesus' original masterpiece, we must adjust the lens quickly or lose the picture entirely. The matter is urgent!

Healthy churches consist of loving, growing, joyful, nurturing groups of people joined in a fellowship of grace; saving and edifying souls, increasing and abounding in love; feeding on the word; filled with the Spirit, and impacting culture with lives reflecting Jesus. Good deeds identify them; joyful celebrations of grace, faith, love and hope define their worship. Glowing with good health, they *know* they are the body of Christ on earth. By doing and being what Jesus would be and do, healthy churches function as their builder intended.

The church is sick because it has become something God never intended. We have taken what Jesus built and used it for the wrong purposes. Physical analogies abound. Lungs meant to breathe fresh air forced to continuously inhale toxic smoke; muscles meant to be strong and useful allowed to atrophy; organs designed to digest food forced to deal with drugs or large quantities of alcohol; brains meant to receive and process information forced full of puerile trash. Churches meant to broadcast the good news have become comfortable groups of spectators. Getting well requires stopping the abuse quickly before irreparable damage occurs!

Incompatibility with the ideal embodied in the Word makes the church unwell. Do we want the church to get well? Do we want to see the bride of Christ radiant in all her glory? Do we want to see Zion again towering above the clouds? Do we want Christianity to appear as it really is: visible, credible, desirable and effective? Then we must change course now and steer on the heading given by the Master. This requires *revolution*; an uprising of disciples who refuse to follow false messiahs any longer.

Other voices also call for an uprising. Some call for an ill-conceived revolt that disregards biblical authority in shaping the modern presentation of the church. Others, off track and stuck in their own ruts of tradition and opinion, hotly disagree. Be advised: we don't have time for another issue. We don't have time to fool ourselves into thinking all is well. The times demand honesty! We don't need more extremism from either left or right. What we do need is courage. Courage to compare what we are to what we should be, and guts to do something about it!

Because we dodge our responsibility and fail to influence our culture, Western society slips its moral moorings. Consequently, our civilization drifts toward certain destruction. Unless believers take the helm, it will surely dash to pieces upon the rocky reefs of oblivion. Remember, God's judgment frequently takes the form of surgically removing offending civilizations from their pedestals of humanistic arrogance.

Dreaming of Freedom

Let's dream new dreams. Let visions of a church that truly reflects the New Testament essence fill our heads. Recapture the essence; and restoration of both form and purpose follow. Multiplied billions of souls are in jeopardy. Our responsibility will not go away. We can ignore it, reject it, rename it, or twist it into something else. The responsibility remains. Doomed billions must hear the words that save them.[1] How tragic that we must even be reminded of this! Making Jesus our Lord automatically makes us responsible for reaching others.

> *"Everyone who calls on the name of the Lord will be saved."* How, then, can they call on the one they have not believed in? And how can they believe in the one of whom they have not heard? And how can they hear without someone

> *preaching to them? And how can they*
> *preach unless they are sent? As it is*
> *written, "How beautiful are the feet of*
> *those who bring good news" (Romans*
> *10:13-15).*

As the end of the century looms into sight, the universal church must come to grips with the self-evident truth: *we have failed miserably in our mission.* Entrusted with the means of reaching the lost, heirs and stewards of the gospel have *blown it!* We blindly stumble from the original path marked by the Master to become a "Worship Society."[2] We build buildings and hold "worship services" (a phrase, incidentally, not found in scripture). *Service* in the cause of Christ has only a small part to do with what happens in our church buildings. Elton Trueblood writes,

> It cannot be too emphatically pointed
> out that such "service" (in New
> Testament times-DW) was not remotely
> similar to what we call a "service"
> today, a polite gathering of auditors, sit-
> ting in comfortable pews listening to a
> clergyman and a choir.[3]

As a result, we have lost our central focus: reaching the lost and edifying the saved. The days of revivals and gospel meetings are over but, stubbornly, we keep trying to *make* them work. Someone has defined *insanity* as doing the same things we've always done and expecting different results. If that's true, aren't we victims of *chronic, acute* insanity to continue the same old stuff that becomes less effective with each passing decade? What we're doing is not working because we're not working like Jesus and his apostles.

Wanted: *Radical Christians!*

> Ra-di-cal adj. 1. Of, proceeding from, or
>
> pertaining to the root or foundation;
> essential; fundamental; inherent, basic.
> 2. Thoroughgoing; unsparing; extreme:
> a radical operation; radical measures.[4]

What an interesting word! It comes from the Latin word, *radix*, which means *root*. The Funk and Wagnalls dictionary goes on to say,

> A radical difference is one that springs
> from the root, and is thus constitutional,
> essential, fundamental, organic, origi-
> nal; a radical change is one that does not
> stop at the surface, but reaches down to
> the very root, and is entire, thorough,
> total; since the majority find superficial
> treatment of any matter the easiest and
> most comfortable, radical measures,
> which strike at the root of evil or need,
> are apt to be looked upon as extreme.

I can't think of a better description of the task before us. No more superficial, cosmetic measures! The transformation must be entire, thorough, total! The world needs *radical Christians.* Our world cries for *extreme measures.* For us, this means following a religious *radical* named Jesus.

Radical Christianity is not practiced in a church building. The *National and International Religion Report,* July 25, 1990, quotes Moshe Rosen, executive director of *Jews for Jesus* as saying,

> The problem in the American church is
> a great deal of inreach and not much

> outreach. The Great Commission is
> reversed. The proclaimers of the gospel
> have retreated in sanctuaries, places
> they own and rent. (Instead, Christians
> should be) out on the highways and
> byways of life, (presenting the gospel)
> to people who have not made a decision.

To be radical, we must get to the root of the problem. Jesus never organized or held a 'worship service.' He did not become flesh to preach to the saved inside a building. He came to seek and save the lost. He told us to take up where he left off. We do that by imitating Him.

And so, this book calls those who know that change is essential to courageously agitate for an *urgent, righteous, radical revolt.* The only way to be satisfied with where we are now is to be unaware of where we *should* be. God calls us to rediscover our purpose and destiny as Israel in the days of Hezekiah. Then, after we have fasted and wept and repented, we must surrender ourselves into the hands of Yahweh. He will reshape our surrendered lives into the image of his Son that we might truly become the body of Christ. Then, stand back and behold the power of God as he works among his people!

[1] Acts 4:12

[2] Elton Trueblood, *The Company of the Committed* (New York: Harper & Row, Publishers) 1961 31

[3] Trueblood, Ibid.

[4] Funk & Wagnalls *New Comprehensive International Dictionary of the English Language,* Publishers International Press, Newark, New Jersey, 1982.

2

IN THE FOOTSTEPS
OF OUR LEADER

T he old prophet awakened suddenly. There it was again...that extraordinary dream! Or, was it a vision? Quickly calling for his scribe, he dictates the words and describes the pictures that fill his brain. He thinks, "What strange words are these!"

Moses, the prophets, David, and his fellow psalmists must have entertained similar thoughts as the revelations came. Visions of a coming Messiah placed upon their minds found expression in tongue and pen. Filled with curiosity, they sought to know the subject of such mystical and apocalyptic phrases. Who *is* this one "through whom all the nations of the world" would find blessing?[1] Who is this "man of sorrows," pierced, crushed, chastened, scourged? "Cut off from the land of the living" for our transgressions, healing us and bearing our iniquities?[2] Born of a virgin?...how bizarre![3]

Prophesying hundreds of years after the reign of David, a puzzled Micah predicted another "ruler in Israel" born in David's village of Bethlehem. The words seemed so strange: "His goings forth are from long ago, from the days of eternity."[4] Meanwhile, the Jews expected a militant, revolutionary, messiah, not the Prince of Peace.

The Revolution

To students of prophecy, this powerful, supernatural messiah would bring Israel to a position of religious, social, and military supremacy. Visions of David and Solomon's kingdom made hearts beat faster, pumping blood through militant bodies. A revolution *was* coming; but not the one they expected. A *new* covenant for old; performance ex-changed for transformed hearts. The nations were *included,* not *excluded.*[5] Like the prophets of old he would proclaim God's day of vengeance. But Yahweh anointed *this* prophet to bring good news to the afflicted, hope to the hopeless. He bound up the brokenhearted, comforted the mourners, proclaimed liberty to the captives and release to the prisoners. His business was garlands, gladness and praise.[6]

Four centuries slowly passed before that day in the fullness of time[7] when God joined man in an unlikely setting: primitive, poor, and enemy-occupied Palestine. In three short years, a thirty-year-old tradesman, *revolutionized* the very world he had hurled into the heavens on creation morning.

"Body of Christ" is not an accidental metaphor of the church. The body must be the very *personification* of the Christ; his image,[8] his aroma.[9] "Christ in us" becomes "the hope of glory."[10] Paul sought to be a *replica* of Jesus.[11] His most cherished dream was *knowing* him and *identifying with* him.[12] Is this *our dream?* Do we long to display his magnificence, his love, and his glory to a world bogged down in the quagmire of selfishness? We are his body! Through us a hopeless world sees him, inhales the sweetness of his aroma, beholds his glory and regains hope! We must permeate the senses of the world!

Following Christ is the Christian's highest purpose. We eat it, drink it, breathe it, dream it, walk it and talk it. What does it mean? It means we must *copy* him who, while confining his activities to a tiny geographical area, began *the most significant non-violent revolution in history of humanity!* Think of it! Let it fill our consciousness! The most momentous movement in the universe includes us!

In many places the revolution has stalled. In many others it never really began. Let's get out the jumper cables! Recharged by God's Spirit, you and I can again "press the battle ere the night shall veil the glowing skies!"[13] The earth can "tremble 'neath our tread," again! Embrace the revolutionary spirit of Jesus! Take up the fight!

His revolution began at birth. Not conceived as other men, he was "child by the Holy Spirit,"[14] and announced as the Savior.[15] Herod, frightened by news of his birth, tried to kill God incarnate. A futile, panic-stricken slaughter of innocent children could not reverse God's eternal purpose. Jesus' earthly sojourn became a time of fulfillment of the Law of Moses, Prophets, and Psalms.[16] His life and teaching *stirred* the hearts of those who walked with him. His miracles *convicted* those looking and waiting. First eleven, then twelve men witnessed the resurrected and glorified Christ. Word of the risen Savior changed both them and their world forever.

If no one speaks another word about him, the world, will reverberate with his life until the end of time. His influence, though diminishing in Western culture, will continue by sheer momentum. Humanity however, will continue plunging into the abyss of hopelessness unless *souls are won and lives are changed.* Jesus himself asks, *"However, when the Son of Man comes, will He find faith on the earth?"*[17] One thing for sure, *we hold the answer in our hands.* "Yes, Master, with all the talents and power given us, we will live and work that you *may find faith on the earth!"*

We don't need change; we need sweeping transformation—with *big* brooms! We delude ourselves to think we, in our present condition, continue Jesus' revolution. The high contrast between Jesus' methods and those of today's disciples stuns us. Something must be wrong. We must have missed something. Either we're not listening and watching or we've completely misunderstood. Is it any wonder that we have a *stalled revolution?*

We, the comfortable, have forgotten that we follow one who gave comfort no priority.

We, with our well appointed and air-conditioned homes, have overlooked the one who had no place to lay his head.

We, the socially correct, have ignored him who mingled with sinners and outcasts.

We, who seek first the dollar and its power, have ignored the one who said, "Seek first His kingdom and His righteousness..."[18]

We who work so hard to acquire more free time disregard him who spent the night in prayer.

We, who search for new pleasures and distractions, have dismissed him who came to seek and save the lost.

Our *goals* are different. Our *agenda* is different. Our *motivation* is different. Our *focus* is different. In his Foreword to Frank Tillapaugh's groundbreaking book, *"Unleashing the Church,"* Vernon C. Grounds describes the problem well.

> Today, many churches are introverted, concerned about attracting larger and larger congregations to their pulpit-centered services, increasing their budgets, improving and expanding their facilities while their members remain

afflicted with arthritic spectatoritis.[19]

The actions of Jesus and the apostles stand in absolute contrast to our surface considerations. In these stark *differences* lie the *reasons* for a stalled, ineffective revolution. But here's the good news: in the *correction* of these differences lie the *solutions* for restarting and revitalizing it. These differences, far from being *subtle,* illustrate the tragic transmutation of the way of Christ into something he would hardly recognize as his own. Until Christianity more closely resembles the Christ, until we intensely pursue his excellence, until we passionately seek his image, we will continue at best as an innocuous and bland civic club...a fraternity of Pharisees...a sorority of the self-righteous. How do we change course? It's really pretty simple. Look at the map! Consult the compass! Ask for directions!

As the Twig Is Bent

No matter what area of life, relational, vocational, or recreational, we learn our habits, good and bad, from those who live before us. We approach parenthood and ask, what does a parent do? We observe our parents and other parents around us. We naturally assume we will be good parents if we follow their lead. Unfortunately, this is true only if they *really are* good parents.

In the touching song, "Cat's in the Cradle," the late Harry Chapin's lyrics tell of a father and son relationship much too common in our hurried and distracted world. The son craved his father's attention; wanted to be with his dad; play with him; learn from him. Though continually disappointed by his absentee father who kept promising "a real good time" and never came through, he would always admiringly say, "I'm gonna be like you, Dad." The son grew up and went off to college while his father grew older and lonelier. He began to crave his boy's attention. The young man, however, learned his lessons well. He learned to be a neglectful, absentee son who will likely be the same kind of father. "As the twig is bent, so grows the tree."

When immersed, we made a choice to follow the Master. We asked, "How do we follow Jesus?" We looked around taking note of parents, leaders, and others older in the faith. We naturally assumed that following their lead was following Christ. *We must rid ourselves of this deception.* In reality, we follow Christ by *knowing* him. First-hand observation, though impossible, would be wonderful. We do, however, have the recorded observations of those whose lives he impacted.

The Word, and those guided by it thus become our source of knowledge about Jesus. Tired, ineffective, self-satisfied, and inept pew-potatoes can only serve as bad examples. Those with no sense of mission or urgency are appalling role models. Those whose love has grown too cold to even warm a pew; are nothing like the purposeful, focused, Son of God. Filled with fervent, compelling love, he is the leader whose footsteps we seek.

Our God is not a neglecting, absentee father. As his children, we exist as the most completely blessed people in the world. Instead of turning us into robots, he gives us every advantage. He lived where we live, sharing the trials and temptations nipping at our heels as we run the race before us. He revealed himself in his word and gave us a way to live. We cannot plead ignorance. We cannot claim to be misled. Through the knowledge of Jesus Christ, God has given us everything we need to live well and die right. He made the alternatives clear: Life or death. Glory or punishment. *The choices are ours.*

Whether you speak Swahili or Urdu, your value system finds its basis either in the world or in the spiritual realm—in the flesh or in the Holy Spirit. Attempts to combine the two sources or to select aspects of each are doomed to failure. They are oil and water, gasoline and fire. Choose one or the other because they *won't mix!*

It's an old story. Your offspring come to you with the ancient whine, "Aw Mom/Dad, everybody else gets to _____! I never get to do *anything!*" Israel wanted a king because "Everybody else gets to have a king!"[20] They ditched the covenant of Yahweh and "Followed worthless idols and themselves became worthless. They imitated the nations around them although the Lord had ordered them, 'Do not do as they do.' (2 Kings 17:15)"

World-based value systems have access to plenty of high octane influence from neighbors, colleagues, friends, parents, teachers, and of course, the media. If we live in a culture that emphasizes the accumulation of more cattle and wives, then we go for those. If our peers value big houses and luxury automobiles, we are likely to work for those objectives.

The mature Christian rejects futile world-based value systems. Nothing the child of God trusts and values comes from the world. We have determined to "No longer live as the Gentiles do in the futility of their thinking" (Ephesians 4:17). Since we follow Christ, we value what he values. What is important to him is important to us. His purpose is our purpose. Since doing God's will was essential to him, it is essential to us. Everywhere he went, he brought division and a crisis of faith to those who observed and heard.[21] Rest to the weary and burdened? Yes, we do that too! Serving others? Seeking and saving the lost? That's us! Good news to the afflicted! Liberty to the captives! Abundant life! I *love* this job!

We follow one with zero doubts about his identity and purpose. He knew *who* he was and *why* he was here. He came to usher in a world revolution. As revolutionaries, we admire, respect, and imitate our leader. To ignore the example of his urgency and commitment would be foolhardy. To overlook his total commitment to his mission jeopardizes ours. True disciples never require begging or intimidation. They eagerly join the cause. They strain for battle with Satan. They are impatient for victory.

Revolution? *What* Revolution?

Some who have dropped off to sleep need a "wake-up call." Others need a full-fledged resurrection with trumpets and shouting. God's frozen people will always give a cold reception to suggestions of change. On the other hand, those who love Jesus and his church, who weep over her tragic captivity, who mourn because of her inertia, must rise in *revolt*.

My dictionary gives *revolt* two definitions. "**1** A throwing off of allegiance and subjection; an uprising against authority; a rebellion or mutiny; insurrection. **2** An act of protest, refusal, revulsion, or disgust."[22] Clearly, this revolution calls for all of the above! We must *throw off* denominational, traditional, and congregational allegiances.[23] We must *totally reject* subjection to those not subject to Christ; be they parent, spouse, teacher, preacher, or leader.

These ties are strong. These influences are powerful and compelling. Do we have the courage to sustain a *new* allegiance? Other than loving concern, we owe them nothing! We owe God everything! We recognize no other authority than almighty God. His kingdom is our only goal. His glorification is our only purpose.

This revolution calls for new and radically different

perspectives. Beyond reformation or even restoration, it summons us to divest ourselves of everything not directly related to our purpose of glorifying God. For example, no building, however glorious, can glorify him who does not dwell in temples made with hands.

Dictators posing as church leaders *detract* from his glory.

Contrived and artificially pumped-up worship *betrays* him.

Our characteristic arrogance and isolation *devalue* him.

Our failure to make diligent efforts to give Jesus to our communities *disgraces* him.

Our reluctance to morally impact our culture *degrades* him.

But look at the Son! Notice how he glorifies his God and Father. *We must become the Son!* Frank Tillapaugh says it well:

> The local church is the visible manifestation of this Body, ordained by God to carry His witness and to be salt and light to the world. In too many instances we have abrogated this responsibility to a needy world and have turned inward, ministering only to ourselves. We are
>
> "the church of the Living God, the pillar and ground of the truth."[24]

Jesus took his message to the synagogues. We must take his message to the places where believers gather...no matter what denomination.[25] Jesus took his message to the streets. We must take it to the shopping malls, open markets, and crossroads. Jesus became involved in human crises of suffering.

We must seek to alleviate the suffering of those among us. We must become concerned about the health and welfare of families. When someone tells us we can't do it, we must have the courage to say, "You hide and watch!" and *mean* it.

Kicking Status in the Quo

This calls for *revolutionary methodology.* We must funnel money away from bottomless pits such as opulent buildings with plush appointments and fund projects promoting the cause of Christ by addressing human suffering and need. Such methods may require not having a paid minister for every little thing. Instead of ostentatious monuments to ourselves, we may need to build inexpensive, functional buildings. As we discuss later in the book, this may mean doing without buildings altogether! Cooperation with other fellowships will often be necessary as we provide help to the hurting.[26] When those appointed as leaders of a congregation block innovative but scriptural approaches, we should gently urge their repentance. Failing that, we should have the bravery to urge their resignation that we might appoint leaders truly interested in following Christ. Now, you may call this *rebellion,* and you are right. Rebellion to ungodly and destructive forces threatening to sabotage our mission requires no apology *Surrender* to the will of God means *rebellion* to the status quo of Satan.

This is not new! The *urgent revolution* began as the Word became flesh and dwelt among us.[27] That movement toppled kingdoms, changed hearts and minds, repeatedly cleansed society, established nations, destroyed barriers, lifted the downtrodden and oppressed, inspired countless acts of mercy and kindness, provided hope to the hopeless, and, most especially and importantly, saved countless souls from the fires of eternal punishment.

Can it happen again? The power and the provisions are as accessible as Bible study and prayer. But do we have disciples with the will and commitment to follow *in the foot-steps of our leader?*

He stands watching his
disciples from heaven's gate.
A tear escapes his eyes.
Why are you crying
Master?
Is it joy or sorrow?

[1]Genesis 12:2; Galatians 3:8

[2]Isaiah 53

[3]Isaiah 7:14

[4]Micah 5:2

[5]Isaiah 2:2; Genesis 22:18

[6]Isaiah 61:1-3

[7]Galatians 4:4

[8]Romans 8:29

[9]2 Corinthians 2:14-16

[10]Colossians 1:27

[11]Galatians 2:20

[12]Philippians 3:7-11

[13]John H. Yates and Ira D. Sankey, "Faith is the Victory," *Songs of the Church,* Howard Publishers, West Monroe, La., 71291, 1977, Song, no.97

[14]Luke 1:25; Matthew 1:18

[15]Luke 2:10,11

[16]Luke 24:44

[17]Luke 18:8

[18]Matthew 6:33

[19]Vernon C. Grounds in his Foreword to Frank R. Tillapaugh's, *Unleashing the Church,* Regal Books, Ventura, California 93006, 1982, p.5

[20]1 Samuel 8:5

[21]Matthew 10:34,35; John 9:39

[22]Funk & Wagnalls *New Comprehensive International Dictionary of the English Language,* Publishers International Press, Newark, New Jersey, 1982, p. 1079

[23] Commitment to Christ, however, demands commitment to His body, especially the one with which we have agreed to work and worship.

[24]Frank R. Tillapaugh, *Unleashing the Church,* Regal Books,Ventura, California, 93006, 1982, p. 21

[25]The "watchdogs of the faith" will not like that. They will write us up in their little yellow papers and imagine that they are righteous for doing so.

[26] Such as Crisis Pregnancy Centers and efforts to repeal ungodly laws and ordinances.

[27]John 1:14

3

THE NEW TESTAMENT WAY

The Issues

He was an earnest fellow doing a good job preaching for a church that had been around for a hundred and twenty years. As we sat with our iced tea in the parsonage parlor getting acquainted, he turned to me with a serious look on his face and asked, "Dwight, what do you think about the issues?" With great wisdom I responded, "What issues?" Looking amazed he replied, "You know...the issues facing the church." I suppose my expression betrayed my gross ignorance. Out of pity, I am sure, he proceeded to educate me on who was up to what and how. He shared with me the dangers "they" posed to the church. He assured me that those brethren with their "uncertain sounds" were abandoning the New Testament pattern. I nodded to indicate I understood, but was thinking, "What has this got to do with *your* work and the mission of *this* church?"

Several years later, I spoke to a group of teachers in a medium-sized congregation. An elder was handing out a thick, hard-back book as an award to outstanding teachers. I thought, "How nice! A book of encouragement these teachers will treasure and place in their bookshelves with pride." During a lull in the proceedings, I ambled over to thumb through the book. It was one of the most negative diatribes I have seen in a long time. These hard-working teachers now had a book filled with the names, alleged misdeeds, and errors of preacher after preacher. I was flabbergasted! Offhandedly, I remarked to a person sitting next to me, "Seems like an odd sort of book to hand out as an award. Is it supposed to be encouraging?" Somehow, the wife of the man handing out the awards over-heard me (not hard to imagine since I have a voice that carries all too well) and proceeded to rat on me to her husband. Soon a red-faced, angry man was speaking to me through clenched teeth, "So you think this is a funny book to hand out to people, huh?"

I had two choices: (1) cut for the door (but they hadn't given me my check yet) or (2) try to discuss the matter. The latter choice also seemed out. He was obviously several degrees hotter than normal "discussing temperature." And so, again mustering great wisdom borne of years of courageous mission work among the natives of the Dallas/Ft. Worth Metroplex, I asked, "What's the purpose of this book anyway? It just tears folks down." I don't suppose he'd ever been asked that question before so it took a bit of sputtering before he came out with this little jewel: "Well, how will you know *who not to invite to speak* if you don't know who the false teachers are? I replied, "Since when do we need somebody's book to tell us that? We all have *Bibles* don't we?" That was too much for the tattle-tale wife who started it. She pulled him off with "Come on, Archie, you don't want to have a stroke over this!" Soon after, I too departed...no doubt permanently.

Here's the point: *we have missed the point!* We have let "the issues" over shadow the main issue: *without the gospel, millions and millions are hopelessly lost.* Others continue to leave the faith in sheer disgust and discouragement over constant infighting. Because some church over in East Piney Slab starts using grape soda in the Lord's Supper does not constitute an obligation on my part to "mark" them and warn the rest of the brotherhood about the "carbonated brethren," lest one of those false fosterers of fizzyness be inadvertently invited to speak at one of our faithful bastions of pure (albeit flat) Welch's grape juice. Haven't we anything *better* to do?

Can you imagine the apostles, prophets, evangelists, pastors, and teachers of the first century spending their time and energy like we do? Buildings, budgets, worship assemblies, professional staffs and "high-maintenance members" drain away our time. Elders are burdened with administration and sorting through piles of requests for support. Often they are too distracted to see to the needs and welfare of the flock.

Our primary emphasis is upon our assemblies: their quality, length, attendance, and the amount of money taken up during them. You can look until your eyeballs fall out and not find the same emphasis among those who walked with Jesus.

Eyes brimming with tears, they saw him die.

Eyes blurred with confusion, they saw the empty tomb.

Eyes wide with wonder, they touched his pierced side and hands.

Eyes filled with awe, they watched him ascend into the heavens.

With single-eyed *passion,* one purpose consumed them: to tell every human being what their eyes had seen and their hands had touched.[1] Now it is our turn to continue their rendition of God's lovesong.

Fortress or Army?

We seem confused. Is the called-out body of Christ a

group of people offering escape from the world outside... "a home within the wilderness, a rest along the way?"[2] Is it a familiar group of friends where we find acceptance, validity, and refuge? More and more we use the word *family* to refer to the koinonia (fellowship of saints). A positive word for most of us, it conjures up feelings of comfort, safety, and well-being. When I think of the church as a family I think of being valued, nurtured, and perhaps, even cherished. In this day of rootless nomadic families, the church replaces the extended family left hundreds, sometimes thousands, of miles behind. We must, however, have a much larger view of the body of Christ or be crippled by our incomplete and inadequate understanding. Yes, we are God's family, but our workday continues. We are toiling with our brothers and sisters in the fields of God. We yet have work to do.

Isn't the church an *army* composed of sanctified men and women who "go marching in" confronting and battling the Satanic forces of darkness? Isn't the church an aggressive and militant band of Christian soldiers "marching as to war? "[3] To whom do we sing, "Soldiers of Christ, arise!"?[4] If you look around during an assembly, however, how do you think most members see the church? Do they see a group of focused, passionate disciples resplendent in the brilliance of Jesus?

The purpose of a family is to nurture and launch strong children into the world. We must go *beyond* the notion of refuge to take an active, offensive stand against the kingdom of darkness. We need *renewed awareness* of our mission and *renewed determination* to fulfill it. And, we need it on an *individual, rank and file* level. Nothing changes, however, if we fail to translate renewed awareness and determination into *actions* and *attitudes*.

People who see the church as a fortress perceive our role as *defensive,* the legacy of years of *reacting* to Satan instead of *acting* against him. Tragically, most churches fit this description. If we insist on a fortress mentality, we'd best be on guard lest we are besieged behind the walls! Leave the fortress! Engage the enemy! Satan is not content with outside attacks. He also raids *inside* the fortress, diverting our attention. We forget he's *outside* raping, pillaging, ravaging the countryside, and plundering the hearts of men and women. Listen! Can you hear the screams of terror and pain? We must rescue them! We must respond to their cries for help! The children of light must immediately take the offensive and assault the prince of darkness. While we whine about the length of the "service," Satan savors his freedom to devour. While we sit cushioned in air-conditioned comfort drugged by the droning sermon, Satan is wide awake and raising hell.

Assembly

We prove our "fortress idea" of the church by emphasizing our own needs when we assemble. The majority of our social contacts and activities happen within the walls of the building (fortress) and among the members. Assemblies become a means within themselves. We measure *faithfulness* by *attendance, success* by *numbers:* dollars collected, warm bodies attending. *God is the fortress* and *we are the army!* As Luther put it, "A mighty fortress is our God, a bulwark never failing."[5]

It is imperative that we get our assemblies back in proper focus. Where did we get this tendency to make assembly *the definitive event* of the Christian week? How did it achieve this all-important status? How did it come to be the function that everyone prepares for and works toward all week long? Who gave it the position of "leading spiritual indicator" determining the "faithfulness" of the individual disciple and the general health and welfare of the church? Is this what the

Bible teaches?

If we make a non-scholarly, cursory study of assembling in the Scriptures, here is what we learn:

1. Under the Law,assembling as such took place during sacrifices, feasts and other religious gatherings as a means to an end, never an end within itself.

2. The Sabbath was, by law, a day of assembling along with other appointed feasts and times of sacrifice.(Leviticus 23:3). Sabbath assembly for the purpose of corporate reading, study and prayer originated, it seems, as an expediency during Babylonian captivity.

3. Christians are commanded to not forsake the assembling of ourselves together. Assembly is essential because there exists no other way to commune around the Lord's table. We cannot teach and admonish one another in singing without assembling. Only assembly expedites public reading and prayer. As a convenience, and by example, assembly provides a time to collect money to do the Lord's work.[6] Assembly affords opportunities to encourage and stimulate one another to love and good deeds.

4. In 1 Corinthians 14, Paul recognized evangelistic potential, but the purpose of assembly is edification, not evangelism.

5. Christians assemble to fulfill a purpose, not meet a requirement.

What does this tell us? It tells us our heavy, almost exclusive emphasis on assembly dangerously borders on the extra-biblical. But what *harm* does it do? Let's be candid for a moment and honestly consider. Can you see that we have homed-in on matters concerning assembly at the expense of matters that are just as weighty? Elton Trueblood wrote,

> "When we think of religion as what
> transpires on Sunday morning, the harm

> lies in the tendency to suppose that what
> goes on at other times, in factories and
> offices, is not equally religious."[7]

This study also tells us that attempts to pin most of our evangelistic hopes on worship assemblies that identify with with the unchurched are misguided. Connecting with the unchurched must not depend primarily on luring them into our assemblies and impressing them with how contemporary we are.

Celebrative times of assembly that edify the saints as a first objective will, by their very nature, be impressive to visitors. When the visitor/outsider sees the saints loving and encouraging each other while lifting praises to God they will be moved. When they see the children of God tenderly remember the sacrifice of Jesus their hearts will be touched.

Misplaced emphasis on assembly has cost us outreach and influence. The result of this "indoor religion" has been a largely invisible gospel persisting in our communities more like a benign lump than an active, penetrating leaven.

All my life I heard Hebrews 10:25 quoted as a command to be present at the assemblies of the church:

> *"...not forsaking our own assembling*
> *together, as is the habit of some but*
> *encouraging one another; and all the*
> *more, as you see the day drawing near."*
> *(NASB)*

Typically, only verse 25 was quoted. Until I began my own study I never realized the real emphasis of this passage. According to the Hebrew writer, assembling provides time for encouragement to faithfulness and provocation to love and good deeds. When our time together is over, I should be filled with a burning desire to bring the love of Jesus into my family and world. Our sharing together supplies a means (encouraging, edifying, stimulating) to an end (love and good deeds), never an end within itself.

In our concern to be scriptural in the form of corporate worship, we have lost our concern to be scriptural in *purpose*. Designed as a time for rallying, assembly equips us and fills us with motivation to become good soldiers in God's army. Here we enflame each other with zeal! We mutually stoke fires of commitment. We kindle each other's love and spotlight opportunities for good deeds. Never designed as a place where people passively observe worship rituals and listen to sermons, scriptural assembly renews our sense of mission and our passion to fulfill it.

Pressing the Battle

"Sense of mission" simply means our focus on the job we've been given to do. It means becoming so preoccupied with the task at hand that peripheral, unrelated matters don't dominate our attention. We're too busy to fuss and fight. We're too busy *doing* to spend any more time *talking*. We have too much to do to be drawn into concentrating on problems and licking wounds. Bringing Christ into our family, business or classroom relationships excites and energizes us.

Our mission and purpose, in short, are the same as Jesus'. While we cannot become the atoning sacrifice, we *can* become "living sacrifices."[8] Though not called to die upon a cross, we *are* called to take our cross daily.[9] We *are* called to be crucified *with* him[10] and die to self.[11] We become a channel of blessing bringing rest to the weary and heavily burdened.[12] We bring abundant life,[13] grace, mercy, and peace to a world starving for comfort, consolation, and encouragement.[14] Most of all, we bring escape from sin and its guilt.[15] Why did my savior come to earth? *For the same reason we are here.* What is the "New Testament Way?" Following him who said, *"I am the way."*

Following Christ means action! It means individual Christians exercising their gifts. It may be something simple like taking a meal to the family with sick kids across the street. It may be something as complex as taking the initiative to help open a halfway house or crisis pregnancy center to help stem abortion's tide. It may be something as simple as getting involved in small-group evangelism. It may be something more complex like leading that group. Act! Get together with others with the readiness to do battle. Brainstorm about strategy and how to implement it. And please, *please,* don't wait to be led! No longer be content to passively let Satan have his way, get into the action! Don't be afraid to make mistakes or fail. Our adequacy comes from God.

This can't be done in front of the shimmering one-eyed god sitting in our dens and living rooms. Christians are not immune to "television abuse." Most of the programming is far away from the mind and spirit of Christ. As soldiers, we refuse to become entangled in stuff distracting us from our mission.[16] When becoming living sacrifices, comfort and convenience are not considerations.[17] A chosen race and a royal priesthood proclaims the excellencies of Jesus Christ.[18] March out of the fortress to battle with the world forces of this darkness! Press on toward ultimate victory under the banner of the Lamb of God who takes away the sins of the world.

[1] 1 John 1:1

[2] Elizabeth Clephane and Frederick C. Maker, "Beneath the Cross of Jesus," *Songs of the Church,* Howard Publishers, West Monroe, LA, 71291, 1977, Song no. 38.

[3] Sabine Baring-Gould and Arthur Sullivan, "Onward, Christian Soldiers," *Songs of the Church,* Howard Publishers, West Monroe, LA., 71291, 1977, Song no. 418.

[4] Charles Wesley and Wm. B. Bradbury, "Soldiers of Christ, Arise," *Songs of the Church,* Howard Publishers, West Monroe, LA, 71291, 1977, Song no. 480.

[5] Martin Luther, Hymn: "A Mighty Fortress is Our God."

[6] 1 Corinthians 16:1,2

[7] Elton Trueblood, *The Company of the Committed,* Harper & Row, Publishers, New York, 1961, page 9.

[8] Romans 12:1

[9] Luke 9:23

[10] Romans 6:6; Galatians 2:20

[11] Colossians 3:2,3

[12] Matthew 11:28

[13] John 10:10

[14] Hebrews 4:16; John 14:17; Philippians 2:1

[15] Romans 7:14-8:3

[16] 2 Timothy 2:3,4

[17] Romans 12:1,2

[18] 1 Peter 2:9

4

GAINING CREDIBILITY

The dining-room table is a powerful tool in God's hands! During our missionary days, we enjoyed sharing evening meals with many couples. A particular Australian couple especially comes to mind. Even though we were dirt-poor, we knew how to eat cheap. We sat around our rag-tag table salvaged from somewhere. Even though the top was covered with linoleum, if you put your best table cloth over it, no one could guess the ugly truth. The chairs we sat on were outcasts from the University of Adelaide, obviously designed to keep the student painfully awake. One could not sit for very long without a strange numbness creeping into the posterior region.

We had already enjoyed a simple feast prepared by Brenda, my bride of seven years. Since this was the second or third time we had eaten with this couple, they were beginning to relax in our spartan little house in spite of the "chairs from hell."

After dinner, over coffee and dessert, the visiting wife suddenly blurted out, "I can't figure it out! What's different about your home?" Brenda and I exchanged knowing glances. Wow! This was exactly what we wanted them to say! Hoping the conversation would go the right direction, we asked,

"Exactly what do you mean, 'different'?" "We feel so comfortable here," she said, her husband nodding agreement. "You make us feel as though you really care about us and we've only known you for such a short time." Beginning at this point, we told them how Jesus made our home "different."

Eventually, we had the pleasure of immersing them into Christ. That was many years ago. We have always tried to make our home an example of what it means to be a "Christian family." I am ashamed to say we have often miserably failed to do this. I'm really telling what we have *endeavored* to do. When successful, we gain enough credibility to share Christ with precious souls.

How do we get people to take us, our Lord, and our gospel seriously? The credibility of Christianity is at an all time low. A major reason: Christians don't seem any different from anybody else. Why would anyone want to be part of a way of life that makes no difference? Donald Posterski puts it this way:

> What incentive is there to investigate a faith that has lost its reputation for making a difference? If the modern brand of Christianity is not producing behavior change, in all honesty, what do Christians have to offer those who are not Christians?[1]

People must see the difference Jesus can make in our homes, our schools, businesses, and other relationships. Primitive Christianity exploded on the scene of paganism because of the contrast it provided. They had inherited a futile way of life but Christianity promised meaning, purpose and forgiveness packaged in simple devotion to one Creator and his only begotten son. Today, the Way must reveal a way of escape for those caught in modern traps of futility. How can we show Jesus to those who need him most?

This process might be summed-up as "earning our right to be listened to." Let me assure you, the world asks, "Why should we listen to you?" They want to see some reason to hear. While there are many ways to provide a reason, one thing for sure: they will not come looking for it. They won't say to themselves, "I believe I'll just go into this church building here and observe Christians for awhile." And yet, our usual M.O. is based on luring people into our buildings.

Why People Listen

Drawing people inside by constructing a nice building, hiring a dynamic young preacher, and trying to look and act like respectable folks has been our strategy for a long time. Slowly, a realization has crept into our brains that we are not growing. We have exchanged peaceful coexistence for growth. Have we forgotten what Jesus said about that?

Blessed are you when people insult you, persecute you and falsely say all kinds of evil against you because of me. Rejoice and be glad, because great is your reward in heaven for in the same way they persecuted the prophets who were before you.[2]

Woe to you when all men speak well of you, for that is how their fathers treated the false prophets.[3]

We make a serious mistake by equating community acceptance with credibility. When everybody loves us we have ceased to function as the counter-culture we were designed to be.

Let's face it. We haven't been very smart. People are not going to listen to the gospel simply because we are preaching it. We do a bit of advertising, get in our building or some other auditorium, expecting people to beat down the doors to hear our wonderful speeches. Alas, it has never worked that way and it never will! People listened to Jesus because he loved the souls of men and women and they knew it. He proved his concern by the deeds of kindness he performed.[4] He, and those who first followed, earned the right to be heard. Jesus, his apostles and disciples, validated the gospel by their deeds.[5] We still need validation. We still have something to prove!

> When people who call themselves Christians express care and love in this world, their behavior rings with Christlikeness. Caring not only authenticates the claim to be Christian, it awakens people to how beautiful life can be and prompts them to consider the Savior.[6]

We must prove that what we want to give away is worth giving away. How do we do that? By proving ourselves *"to be blameless and innocent, children of God above reproach in the midst of a crooked and perverse generation, among whom (we) appear as lights in the world."*[7]

Susan Maycinik, editor of Discipleship Journal points out that if we are to win the hearts of our communities, we must be known as practitioners of love. She writes, "Secular people listen when Mother Theresa denounces abortion, but only because she captured their attention with a lifetime of selfless service to the poor and dying."[8]

Consequently, Jesus and the apostles heavily stressed good deeds. They taught that the gospel must be seen as well as heard in the lives of his followers. Jesus knows that nobody's going to believe, trust, and obey an invisible Savior.

When converted people preach a valid gospel, the lost will listen to it. It was said of Chrysostom, the ancient preacher of Constantinople, "The gold of his life undergirded the currency of his words."[9] Nice, comfortable buildings, "meaningful" worship services and impressive programs will not get the gospel to them. What will? Lives that are "adorning the doctrine of God in every respect."[10]

Expecting instant acceptance of our message is madness. First we must gain the attention of those we want to listen by letting Christ be seen in us. With enough time and patience, we can cut through the underbrush of suspicion and misunderstanding.

People whose door has been recently knocked by the Mormons, Jehovah's Witnesses, and other cults are not going to roll out the red carpet for another person in a shirt and tie carrying a black briefcase. "Be quiet Martha! Maybe they'll think no one's home. Yes, I know the kitchen floor is cold, but lay there anyway. They might look in the window!"

For these reasons, and because nearly everyone in the developing nations has heard of our religious con artists and their scams, American teachers and preachers are suspect. It would ordinarily take years to live down such an unwarranted and unwanted reputation. It can happen quickly, though, if we are willing to be Jesus in the marketplace. But heed the warning: nothing at all will happen if we confine ourselves to the safety and anonymity of our church buildings.

In every community, we must envision ourselves as outposts of the gospel on the frontier of the kingdom. We must spend time praying, thinking, planning, and scheming about how to gain a hearing. We've got to quit figuring out how to make the trenches more attractive and comfortable *and get out of them.* Charge the forces of evil! Beat back the lines of the kingdom of darkness! Take a higher profile and draw Satan's fire!

Changing the way we think about our community and ourselves is the first step. Adjustments are urgent and necessary! The minds of people in our world are the territory currently occupied by Satan. Their hearts are the battlefields into which we charge with the ultimate weapon: *the gospel.* Our objective: *"We demolish arguments and every pretension that sets itself up against the knowledge of God, and we take captive every thought to make it obedient to Christ."*[11] We're here to snatch them out of the fire,[12] rescue them from the "dominion of darkness," and bring them into the "kingdom of the Son he loves."[13]

Church Buildings: A Help or a Hindrance?

Finally getting a church building built has been a major goal for many a struggling congregation. I personally remember becoming very tired of our public hall in Elizabeth, South Australia. Very often it was necessary to clean up the spilled beer, wine, and vomit left over from the Saturday night revelers who used the same hall. Our kids had to have Bible classes in locker rooms smelling of sweat, liniment, and mud. When it came time to immerse people into Christ in winter, we prayed their faith would never grow as cold as that water! We had some of the quickest winter baptisms on record: "Inowbaptizeyouinthenamevthufathersun'holyspiritamen!" Splash! Whoosh! and outathere!

When we were able to see our way clear to finance a building, we thought we had reached a major milestone. Now we would have a nice auditorium in which to meet, including a baptistery filled with warm water. Now we would have plenty of classroom space for the kids...we could leave stuff on the bulletin boards...no more frying in the summer and freezing in the winter. It would give us an aura of permanence and respectability in the community.

When the building was completed and we were all moved in, something seemed amiss. Attendance for midweek Bible studies dropped. We had fewer visitors. Our enthusiasm seemed to dwindle. Some folks openly admitted that they missed meeting in homes with everyone crammed into someone's living room. They missed the fellowship...the intimate (crowded!) atmosphere. Furthermore, it was harder to attract visitors to a "church" than it was to a public hall or home.

Obviously, looking back from the perspective of intervening decades, seeking the credibility and convenience of a building removed us from the "cutting edge" of evangelism. No longer a struggling congregation on the frontier of the kingdom, we had "arrived." Since those days, I have seen the same thing happen in the United States and, I believe I know the reason: we decided credibility meant a building. The more *magnificent*, the more credibility.

In order to have any influence whatsoever, Christianity must be *visible*, something practiced in the open! Multitudes of passages clearly point out the *public nature* of the religion of Christ. With the exception of the parachurch organizations, we now practice our religion mainly indoors...a place where few outsiders will dare to tread. The rest of the time we anxiously try to blend in. We try to look and act like those among whom we live and work. That's certainly understandable...it is most uncomfortable to do otherwise.

> Of course we are not the only ones try-
> ing desperately to be mainstream...
> (Note, for example, how some of the
> holiness fellowships have moved from
> strictly no make-up to Tammy Faye-like
> excess.) But we have to be honest about
> our longing for respectability. The
> desire to conform is very, very strong.[14]

As a result, outreach and impact on our culture are rare.

The early church grew because it involved those *called* out of their culture. They knew they didn't belong there any-more. Being *different* was part and parcel of their conversion to Christ. They left the futile ways of their forefathers and that meant basic changes in morals and values. The spectacle of their sudden and drastic change of lifestyle was amazing, alarming. Ron Carlson has written, "Christianity stands unique above the world's other religions and philosophies because of the level of change it demands."[15]

In the beginning, Christians had no church buildings to hide in. The light of their life and worship pierced the dark night of paganism. The beams of their faith brightly shim-mered for anyone caring to observe. Many *did observe* and decided to become disciples themselves. Around 200 Tertullian wrote,

> We are a new group but have already
> penetrated all areas of imperial life —
> cities, islands, villages, towns, market-
> places, even the camp, tribes, palace,
> senate, the law-court. There is nothing
> left for you but your temples...We live
> in the world with you. We do not for-

sake forum...or bath...or workshop, or inn, or market, or any other place of commerce. We sail with you, fight with you, farm with you...[16]

In some cities in the United States, we have hundreds of churches and thousands of disciples but, we are *hidden*. Unless someone ventures into our assemblies or is the recipient of our benevolence, he or she may never know we *exist!* It is hard to be lights in the world when our light is hidden behind our church building walls. When we were kids singing "This Little Light of Mine," we sang, "Hide it under a bushel? No! I'm gonna let it shine." Obviously, we have tragically exchanged a building for the bushel. And so, in the cities, Christianity has little impact on morals and values. Our limited media exposure comes across "churchy," and unprofessional. Were it not for God's providence, conversions would be the result of accidental exposure plus pure luck. Walter Obetting has observed:

When the early Christians themselves recount how they learned of the Gospel, they usually confess that their faith was the result of casual contact with that "way of life." Justin Martyr recalled that he was converted to the faith when he saw people willing to die for it in the arena. The pagan Celsus scoffed at the workers in wool and leather, the rustic and ignorant persons who spread Christianity. The work was not done by people who called themselves missionaries but by rank-and-file members.[17]

Are buildings the culprit? Of course not. Attitudes,

however, that lead us to practice our Christianity inside those buildings definitely are. Attitudes of self-righteous exclusiveness and isolationism often result from seductive desires for comfort and convenience.

We need to ask serious questions about the advisability of having buildings at all. In places where the church is too large for a house and public space is not available, no one could deny the convenience of a building. But in our larger cities, a very good argument can be put against them.

1. The church we seek to emulate met in homes and public places.

2. Buildings are not "neutral ground" and many non-churched are very reluctant to enter one.

3. Millions of dollars are tied up for many years in erecting and maintaining buildings. This is money urgently needed elsewhere to fulfill our mission.

4. Buildings encourage us to lose touch with the marketplace.

5. Buildings stifle fellowship of small groups. Many congregations are realizing this and establishing "small group ministries."

6. Buildings perpetuate erroneous concepts about "holy places." Many refer to the building as "the church."

Am I suggesting that we sell our buildings and meet in auditoriums, convention centers and public halls? Am I proposing that we use some of the money we save to rent offices and classroom space in busy public places like shopping malls? Do I think we need to take what's left of the money and open crisis centers, food banks and do other acts of mercy? Perhaps. Am I suggesting that instead of building buildings we do everything we can think of to be visible, public and open? Absolutely.

At the very least, we need to convert our poor imitations of cathedrals from "holy ground" to public places. Let the community use them. Let them become centers for dealing mercifully with those caught in the painful pitfalls of life, centers of constant activity for Jesus!

Calithumpians, Confusion and Credibility

Maintaining the trappings of a parent denomination can also cause a hemorrhage of credibility. Personally, I have no interest in promoting or defending any fellowship except that of Jesus. My loyalty to any fellowship ends where human traditions begin. I can't think of anything better than simply divesting ourselves of loyalty to traditions identifying us as one denomination (fellowship, group) or another. Identification with Christ should be our only aspiration.

We hinder the gospel by the exclusive use of one name, be it a name found in Scripture or some other designation. The apostle Paul deplored the exclusive use of a particular name as being divisive or otherwise counterproductive.[18] Why not just be the Church? Why not just identify ourselves as the fellowship of Christ that assembles in a certain area?

The minute we identify ourselves with a specific tradition, we instantly lose credibility with those who've had a negative experience with it. For example, if a devout Calithumpian once told your granny she was going to hell, she will probably never attend a Calithumpian church again, and will divorce Grampaw if he does. Calithumpians would best not use that name when doing mission work in her neighborhood.

Today, thankfully, denominational distinctions are fading. More and more believers are referring to themselves as Christians only. It is wonderful to see commitment to Jesus transcending denominationalism because the urgent revolution cries for love and loyalty so strong that unity is more important than denominational uniqueness.

Promoting and validating the incarnation of Jesus[19] must be top priority. Those insisting on denominational promotion while looking in the tear-streaked face of an unreached world have much to answer for.

Indeed, the unreached world bears mute testimony to the destructiveness of division. By "division" I don't mean *groupings* of Christians along ethnic and linguistic lines. Nor do I refer to groups preferring a particular style of corporate worship. We have to get off each other's backs about stuff that doesn't matter and quit drawing lines of fellowship over every difference of opinion! Yet, care must be taken that such groupings do not become yet another form of division.

Neither passive, monastic nor mystical, the religion of Christ, is an aggressive, yet simple way of life practiced by people who live in the world. Jesus came to live among mankind, not isolated in some spiritual ghetto. He did not require people to search for him in some synagogue, temple or shrine. Except for times of prayerful regeneration, he sought people where they lived and worked. His love and compassion for them was, after all, the reason he became flesh and blood.[20] His good works and mercy gave credence to the message he

lived and shared. If we continue his works of goodness and mercy, the body will have the same credibility.

Indeed, he has cast his mantle upon us, his followers. Do you feel it as it covers your shoulders? Wrap it around you tightly and draw power from it until the day when you can echo His last words on the cross, "It is finished."

[1] Donald C. Posterski, *Reinventing Evangelism*, InterVarsity Press, Downers Grove, Illinois, U.S.A. 1989, p.24

[2] Matthew 5:11,12

[3] Luke 6:26

[4] Acts 10:38

[5] Mark 16:17-20

[6] Posterski, p.42

[7] Philippians 2:15

[8] Susan Maycinik, *Discipleship Journal*, Issue Eighty-six, March/April 1995, The Navigators/NavPress, 7899 Lexington Dr., Colorado Springs, Colorado, p. 8.

[9] Christopher A. Hall, *"Letters From a Lonely Exile,"* Church History, Issue 44, p. 30, Published by *Christianity Today*, Inc., 465 Gundersen Drive, Calrol Stream, IL 60188, 1994

[10] Titus 2:10

[11] 2 Corinthians 10:5

[12] Jude 23

[13] Colossians 1:13

[14] F. LaGard Smith, *The Cultural Church*, 20th Century Christian, 2809 Granny White Pike, Nashville, TN 37204, 1992 p. 110

[15] Ron Carlson, *Comatose Christianity*, Christian Communications, PO. Box 150, Nashville, Tennessee 37202, p. 124

[16] Tertullian, Apology, v:6; xxxvii:4,5; xlii:2,3 as quoted by Everett Ferguson, *Early Christians Speak*, pp. 219,220, Sweet Publishing Company, Austin, Texas, 1971.

[17] Walter Obetting, *The Church of the Catacombs*, p. 24

[18] 1 Corinthians 1:10-17

[19] John 17:20ff

[20] Hebrews 2:14

5

WORDS YOU CAN EAT

Floating Heads

Elsie was dead. While I was at the hospital with her family, the little church of which she was a much loved member had gathered to pray in our house. When it seemed obvious that God was not going to heal her, we decided to gather and pray for her easy release. After she quietly slipped away, I called home and told the group that their prayers were answered. My children were young, and this was their first experience with the death of someone they were close to. And so, trying to be a good mother, Brenda explained death to my seven-year-old son and my four-year-old daughter. She reminded them of eternal life and heaven. What a wonderful opportunity to explain both the mystery of death and the hope we cherish as Christians!

Some weeks later the mother of one of Amy's playmates confirmed that Brenda had apparently done a wonderful job. It seems that Amy had explained the death of Elsie to the woman's daughter in very lucid terms! She found it amazing that such a little girl had a clear picture of death and eternal life!

It took four years for the bubble to burst. One day, sitting around the kitchen table discussing heaven, Amy, then eight years old, said, "You know Mum, when I was a little girl, I didn't want to go to heaven when I died."

Brenda, somewhat taken aback, asked, "Really Amy, why not? Heaven's a wonderful place!"

"Well, you remember when Elsie died?"

"Yes."

"You told me that only her *body* had died, and that the part of her that we love the best had gone to heaven. Since it was her *face* I loved, I thought heaven was full of *people's heads floating around!*"

Multiplied examples teach us that when explaining things to children, one must be very careful to choose right words! Effective communication must never be taken lightly with children *or* adults. Seeking to communicate the truths of Christianity is serious stuff!

All of us have experienced the frustration of being misunderstood and/or misinterpreted. The words we choose can either devastate or enrich our relationships. Carelessly chosen words wreck friendships, destroy marriages, break alliances, and terminate partnerships. On the other hand, poets and song writers know carefully selected words whispered to the object of one's affection can win love. Solomon was right! "A word aptly spoken is like apples of gold in settings of silver."[1] Rudyard Kipling was never more on target than in a 1923 speech when he said, "Words are, of course, the most powerful drug used by mankind."

Because of a combined love for words and people (most of the time), I enjoy preaching the gospel. As the years go by, I see words produce a deeper love for Jesus, his teachings, and the good news of his atoning sacrifice. As I work with precious souls and witness the changes Jesus makes in their lives through God's word, I am deeply grateful to be part of the process.

More than the preparation and delivery of sermons or writing books and articles, the term *communication* comes closest to describing my work. Whether chatting with a couple at the dinner table or delivering a speech to larger groups, the challenge of getting the message across thrills and excites me. No artificial "high" can compare to the awareness that God has actually used you to transmit his message between hearts. I see the smile, the nod of the head, the widening of the eyes, the glance at the one beside them; expressions that say to the communicator: "Yes, I understand, I agree." Or, they may be saying, "Wow! That touched me!" or, "Now I see!" If I've done my job, there are indications that an almost magical transaction called *encouragement* or *edification* has taken place. I'll tell you something you may have already guessed; I wouldn't trade places with *anybody! I love* it!

Deaf People and Dogs

I have serious doubts that humans ever sat around in caves grunting at each other. There had to be a better way to say, "Grab your spears, boys, there's a woolly mammoth stuck in the tar pit!" I will easily admit, however that communication consists of more than mere words. Words are essential, but combining them with movement, posture, and gesture says so much more.

Friends and family members know how to communicate with touches, facial expressions, sighs and laughter. Lovers can speak volumes by gazing into each other's eyes. But how did they attain this sublime non-verbal level? That's right, *words:* conversations, notes, cards, letters, telephone calls, etc.

Words, however, are not always vocally expressed. For example, I enjoy watching the deaf communicate, especially in a deaf church. The city of Adelaide, South Australia, has a whole congregation of the deaf. While I was a young evangelist there, we had times of worship together. With their fluid and fluent hand motions, they sing, teach, preach, and enjoy fellowship. If you are one of the few hearing persons in their assembly, you will hear the swishing of clothing as arms and hands slap, pop and click to arrange thoughts in the form of words. Because of their expressive faces, you can almost understand what they cannot covey by audible speech. Such high level communication gives us huge advantages over the next highest forms of animal life. Because we humans share our thinking via words, we can almost become a "collective mind." When we *fail* to communicate or encounter barriers to effective communication, the consequences are usually destructive. Witness the confusion of languages at the Tower of Babel. After the flood (Genesis 7 and 8), all the nations used the same language. One group of people who settled in the land of Shinar (present day Iraq) learned how to bake brick. They decided to build a huge tower "whose top will reach into heaven." This displeased God and he decided to "confuse their language (Genesis 11:1-9)."

People who cannot or will not communicate are impossible to work with. And so the work stopped on the tower and the people scattered "abroad over the face of the whole earth."

"Joe, hand me that trowel, would you?"

"Sladurp vet yano cumi patooi!"

"Say *what?* Have you been into the fermented barley juice again?"

"Shimee, shimee coco pop, sha-na-na a kiddleat-ivy-too."

Parents have experienced such difficulties since time

began, especially when we say something like, "Clean up your room" or, "Do the dishes." Just about the time we begin to understand the current teen lingo, a whole new set of words, some of which have opposite meanings, make their appearance.

Relationships are the proving grounds for our communication expertise. Without effective skills, marriages, friendships, partnerships and other alliances will not long survive. In our groups and assemblies, the maintenance of spiritual health depends upon our ability to transmit thoughts and ideas from one person to another. his being true, both the *ways* and the *means* of communicating the gospel are *vitally important.* To say, "I love you," to someone in the expressionless monotone of a robot will never touch that person (unless perhaps you are speaking to another robot). But to say, "I love you," with the emphasis and inflection of a lover can open a path to the heart. Knowing this, how can we be so careless in the way we send the most important message ever to enter human ears?

Some with an almost cavalier "take it or leave it" attitude toward their hearers, have erected substantial, sometimes impassable barriers. It's like the food we leave out for our dog, Cedric. He sniffs at it and then walks away in protest. You can almost hear his doggy brain thinking, "Where did they *get* this stuff? I'd rather eat a road-killed armadillo than this mixture of sawdust and cow hooves!" We know that he'll eventually get hungry enough to eat it, but right now he can take it or leave it. When we bought the stuff, fine cuisine was not our chief concern. "$3.95 for forty pounds? We'll take it!" But people are not dogs! We must choose our *language* carefully for *palatability.* Can people swallow what we say or do they choke on the barbs? Does a sour taste obscure spiritual nutrition? Does an ugly presentation hide the beauty of the food?

When I was a beginning preacher, we had an elderly

sister in the congregation who kept insisting that Brenda and I make some visits with her to the local backsliders. She indicated that she was willing to instruct us in the fine art of restoring the erring. I will never forget a visit we made to the home of a member who had not attended for years. After we finished the obligatory talk about the weather, it was time to come to the purpose of our visit. I began by mentioning that we surely would like for he and his wife to start attending again. No sooner had we spoken those words than the older sister said, "Yes, you need to get right with the Lord, brother! Heaven is too precious, Hell is too hot and eternity is too long to take any chances!" With that, our visit was over. We were politely shown the door, our mission sabotaged by well intended but poorly chosen words.

With the salvation of souls at stake, the *words* we use getting the gospel to the lost demand our most urgent attention. We neglect the problem of *how* we preach to ourselves and those who hear us at our own eternal peril. I had a teacher who told me "Contact is more important than tact." If that means a *license* to be tactless, I emphatically disagree. We must pour out the water of life, not spit it in people's faces. The bread of life cannot be force-fed. If we fail to exercise *tact* in the process of making *contact*, we might as well preach to brick walls. If, in the operation of transmitting the gospel, we make folks angry, will they receive our transmission? Doesn't that make contact *and* tact of equal concern? Let me suggest we do something seldom done. *Let's examine the way Jesus did it!*

Hunting Deer and Shooting Cows

Some of my fellow-communicators who downplay the importance of diplomacy like pointing to Jesus as he spoke to the religious leaders of his era. His scathing comments about their sham and hypocrisy scorch the pages on which they are recorded. I've heard it said that if we don't speak this way to people involved in religious error, we're being "soft on false teachers." These folks think we ought to be out there "calling a spade a spade" and challenging the scoundrels to debate. Well, hang on a minute! We need to take a second look at situations in which Jesus reprimanded people. Then, we need to notice how he spoke to those who "had ears to hear."

Let's acknowledge that when Jesus used such terms as "hypocrites," and "whitewashed tombs," and "generation of vipers," he was speaking to people whose hearts were exposed by their actions and speech as insincere show-offs more interested in the praise of men than the honor of Yahweh. They "searched the scriptures" but didn't act like it. No doubt the same kind of people abound in the religious world of today. No doubt they need a full dose of the same medicine Jesus was giving the Pharisees. And yes, on occasion they will say and do things that prove they are the scribes and Pharisees of our day. However, *we'd better make sure we know what kind of critter we're shooting at!* What a foolish mistake to be so trigger-happy that we are like someone who goes hunting for deer and winds up shooting the rancher's cows!

Jesus had "x-ray vision of the heart." Singling out hypocrites was no trouble at all. We, on the other hand, must observe and listen to each individual long enough to make quite sure we know what we're doing! Sometimes we resemble a berserk gunman who gets mad at his boss and starts shooting every fellow-employee in sight! The bullets, like careless words, kill the innocent while the guilty person remains unharmed.

Jesus reserved harsh and sarcastic words for those who had them coming. To others, he was kind and gentle. As he corrects the petulant and distracted Martha, he soothingly responds, *"Martha, Martha..."*[2] To the woman caught in the very act of adultery, Jesus said, *"Neither do I condemn you; go your way; from now on sin no more."*[3]

Jesus' conversation with the Samaritan woman provides an excellent example of how to talk to someone involved not only in religious error, but also a first-rank sinner.[4] If he had called her a heathen (which she was) and an adulteress (which she also was) and used the same language he reserved for the self-righteous religious leaders, she never would have gone into the village crying, "Come and see!" She would've instead been yelling, "Grab a rock, we've got an arrogant Jew out here begging for a good stoning!"

We have many examples: Zacchaeus, the sinful woman with her alabaster vial, Nicodemus, the Canaanite woman, even Judas!

The apostles certainly were not confused about how to speak to people. Paul tells the Ephesians that we are to be speaking the truth in love.[5] He tells the Colossians very plainly how to speak to those outside of Christ.

> Conduct yourselves with wisdom toward outsiders, making the most of the opportunity. Let your speech always be with grace (or, "gracious"), seasoned, as it were with salt, so that you may know how you should respond to each person.[6]

Seasoned words, salted words...words sensitive to the needs of the listeners. Words you can eat!

Timothy is not left in the dark about the fact that "the Lord's bondservant must handle *"those in opposition"* with kindness and gentleness.[7] Some religious contenders seem to be unaware of this passage. To these piously puffed-up pugilists, the opposition exposes a fair target for the full force

of the barbs and slings of their abuse. I'm reminded of buzzards on a perch, eyes scanning the surroundings for a bit of
carrion; always ready to swoop down for another putrid
morsel. Buzzards may not be able to change, but Christians
can and *must*. Peter counseled gentleness and reverence
(respect-NIV) in our readiness to answer questions about our
hope.[8]

How we expect to ever accomplish our mission by
berating others and using sarcasm remains a mystery to me.
Jesus, able to discern their hearts, used both on the Scribes and
Pharisees without solid evidence that he persuaded any to
change. They *were*, however, persuaded to torture him to
death. Jesus seems to have reserved sarcasm and censure to
pronounce judgment, not produce repentance. If our mission
really consists of solidifying the opposition by passing judgment on them, mission accomplished! In plenty of places people have their minds made up about the church. They see us as
narrow-minded and condemning. They have already decided
not to waste any more time messin' with us.

I have preached the gospel in places so polluted by the
poisoned pen and tongue of my predecessors that I shocked the
other preachers in town (and that is not an exaggeration) when
I was friendly with them. What an indictment against those
who claim to follow Jesus! What a setback for those who are
trying to persuade people to leave division behind! Why
would they want to *listen to*, much less be a *part of* what they
perceive to be a judgmental group of sourpusses?

I personally have seen little of the attitude of Jesus and
the apostles in the speech and literature of the religious
"watchdogs." I have seen a lot of self- justification and ratio-
nalization of ungodly behavior. If only they had as much concern for sound doctrine regarding the way they interact with
those in opposition as they do about "the issues!" We must

determine that we will *"speak as the Bible speaks"* in regard to
our *conduct* as well as *content.*

The *Real* Issue

The Holy Spirit speaks clearly about the methods and
attitude of the person assuming the task of correcting those in
error. Arrogantly casting agape aside and acting as hostile
courtroom lawyers interrogating equally hostile witnesses is
not an option. The standard of our conduct toward those outside our own fellowships "goes double" in our relationship to
those within. If we find it impossible to be kind, graceful and
gentle, why work with people at all? If we cannot speak with
humility and respect, then we ought to keep our mouths tightly shut.

Hand in hand, the seed of Adam and the daughters of
Eve walk aimlessly, going nowhere. They stumble over
unseen obstacles, groping in the gloom for gratification and
finding nothing. The night of futility obscures their world.
Pervading the dank atmosphere, an evil presence holds lord-
ship over a domain of darkness. Faith, hope and love are alien
to this bleak nether world. For them, it has ever been thus.
Such an existence seems normal. The spiral of their life
repeats over and over from generation to generation. They are
the walking dead, spiritual zombies slain from the instant of
their first sin.

Across the border in the kingdom of Light, the Lamb of
God rules, seated in the heavenly places on the Throne of
Grace. The citizens of this realm are the sons and daughters of
Abraham. With perfect vision, they run the obstacle course of
life and do not grow weary. With purpose and direction they
fly on wings of eagles in clear, blue skies. Faith, hope and love
fill each hour with joy. They too were dead, but now have been
made alive together with Christ.[9]. And this is only the begin-

ning! The next stop is eternal life of indescribable joys.[10]
Why are some dwelling in Satan's darkness while others are living in God's light? Because of *words*. Not just any words, but words of forgiveness and reconciliation—the utterances of God[11] spoken by Christians living lives that give them credibility. As these words are spoken and understood by those in darkness, the dawn breaks, the gloom is dispelled, and the night of sin flees before the glory of God. To those born again through this living and abiding word[12] the Holy Spirit reveals the course of life and exposes all the obstacles. A lovelier melody than redemption's sweet song has never been sung. Never have so many needed to hear its music!

Fellow Christian, you will never deliver a more urgent message. As we bring this counsel to those who will surely die without it, let us speak carefully chosen words—seasoned, gracious, delicious, words. Then, the barriers of darkness will fall with a mighty crash and the Word who became flesh[13] will pierce the darkness and futility of paganism with *"true light which, coming into the world, enlightens every man."*[14]

[1]Proverbs 25:11
[2]Luke 10:41
[3]John 8:11 (NASB)

[4]John 4:4-42

[5] Ephesians 4:15

[6]Colossians 4:5,6 (NASB)

[7]2 Timothy 2:24,25

[8]1 Peter 3:15

[9]Ephesians 2:1-5

[10]Romans 8:18

[11]1 Peter 4:11

[12]1 Peter 1:24

[13]John 1:14

[14]John 1:9 (NASB)

6

WHAT A MESSAGE!

Our Alien Vocabulary

On the windy plains of the Texas Panhandle a city called Lubbock rises out of the cotton fields. Country music and rock n' roll fans will recognize Lubbock as the home of Buddy Holly, Waylon Jennings and Mack Davis. Institutions of higher learning located there are Texas Technological University and Lubbock Christian University to name two. Another institution of *faster* learning called Sunset International Bible Institute[1] rests in the shadow of these two giants. The Sunset Church of Christ works in cooperation with other interested congregations to provide a tuition-free school designed to prepare men and women for full-time ministry. When I was a student there, the school attempted to cram your brain as full of Bible as two years would allow. After spending five confusing and unsettled years at North Texas State University, I took advantage of the school in 1965. By the time I finished Sunset, I possessed (1)the equivalent of a Master's Degree in Bible, (2)a very technical vocabulary, (3)a strong desire to put out some of what I had taken in and, (4)through no fault of the school, a lot of idealistic nonsense. In other words, I was a highly educated ignoramus.

Six months after graduation found me in Australia trying to preach a very technical and idealistic gospel to ordinary people who barely knew of Jesus. What a joy to share my hard-won knowledge and understanding! It felt good to bless the lives of my hearers with doctrines insuring a closer walk with God. After a few months, however, I detected that something was not quite right. People didn't seem to pay attention as they had at first. What sparse feedback I got indicated that interest in my sermons and lessons was waning. I remember falling to my knees in tears one night asking the Lord to reveal to me what was wrong. Soon I got my answer and boy, was it devastating! My wife became God's messenger as she gently told me, "Honey, I think they just *don't understand what you are saying*. You use some pretty big words and you teach a lot of meat. I think you need to give them *milk first!*" My co-workers and some of the members confirmed what she said. I think I spent the next 24 hours in tears, but it was a watershed in my work as an evangelist.

It really doesn't matter whether I randomly select a person on the streets of Melbourne or Dallas. If I try to talk to him about the "gospel of salvation" and about the Savior who has come to bring "redemption and reconciliation" to mankind, he will likely start trying to get away from this weird person speaking in a strange and unknown tongue. Here's a news flash for you: we Christians have our own language that most outsiders will not be familiar with.

Mike Armour tells about a long-time minister friend who was teaching the gospel to a banker. They had been studying together of a couple of months when, during a particular session, the minister turned to 2 Timothy 3:15 which speaks of the Scriptures as being able to give the wisdom that leads to salvation. As he read the passage, he noticed from the banker's expression that he was not quite following the thought. Since they had already discussed the meaning of "scripture," he knew that wasn't the problem. So, he paused to ask, "Are you having trouble with the word 'salvation' here?" The man admitted he was. "What does salvation mean to you?" asked the minister. The banker pondered this question for a long moment and finally answered, "Well, I don't know...I guess the Salvation Army." Mike goes on to say that there is a whole educated, professional and successful world that finds our "Christian Vocabulary" predominantly alien.[2]

Unfortunately we remain unaware of how exotic our vocabulary seems to those outside. Having dialogue with the ordinary, grass-roots, non-religious person, however, requires speaking their language. Without dialogue, no one will hear our life-changing message. The darkness of helpless futility and hopeless eternity will never see the dawn of meaning and hope. How unspeakable to leave the message unspoken!

Two conditions tend to stand in the way of our fulfillment of Jesus' commission to preach the gospel to every person. First, the church has become ill. SYMPTOMS: the patient is *apathetic* and *sluggish* in her efforts to share the gospel. DIAGNOSIS: acute, chronic *spiritual lassitude*. CAUSE: tired sermons and lethargic leaderships without vision. CURE: daily doses of the Word to build up faith, constant prayer to open our hearts to the Holy Spirit's leading, and regular exercise to shake off stringy cobwebs of indifference. One thing for sure, the church will be in the doldrums anywhere the light of faith and commitment becomes dim in the souls of her members.

Secondly, Christians caught up in the rat-race with the

rest of the world tend to lose sight of the positive, fundamental differences a Christian lifestyle offers to the beleaguered runner. It truly is a "jungle out there" and many have fallen prey to the beasts lurking in the dark. In the thick of such dangerous darkness, however, Jesus is the glowing path to safety. By stepping in the shining footprints of Jesus, lives full of joy, meaning and purpose replace futile, dead-ended pursuits of "happiness."

The message brings good news of guaranteed *eternal* and *indestructible* promises instead of a scramble for trivial and elusive mirages. This message transforms its hearers into the image of the creator and savior while securing the promise of glorious, eternal life.

Over thirty years ago, Elton Trueblood wrote one of the finest books ever penned on what the church *should* be. Among many other excellent and thought-provoking points, he shares an idea particularly germane to understanding the relationship the church sustains to the gospel message:

> The church is intended as a concrete answer to the prayer that laborers be sent forth to the harvest. The Company of Jesus is not people streaming to a shrine; and it is not people making up an audience for a speaker; it is laborers engaged in the harvesting task of reaching their perplexed and seeking brethren with something so vital that, if it is received, it will change their lives.[3]

Lives are changed from *defeat* to *victory*.[4] The "perplexed and seeking" win the victory of certainty and confidence in this life. They win a victory of resurrection over death in the next. This message *empowers* the power-less. Satan's *losers* become Jesus' *winners*.

The very *excellence of the message* kindles our motivation to share it. Perceiving the gospel to be the priceless pearl creates eager passion to share it at all costs. Ignited by the fires of faith, they burn with urgency to announce God's antidotes for poison sin and toxic hopelessness. And, they are "tongue-tied," i.e., their life is tied to their words. In the middle of the bewildering morass of uncertainty, their lifestyle is a beacon of clarity and coherence. Observers see people who, in word and deed ardently proclaim that because the tomb is empty, life is full!

A Message For All People

Jesus knew his ministry and message were the fulfillment of prophecy. In his boyhood home of Nazareth he dared to proclaim that he was the one Isaiah spoke of, saying,

> *The Spirit of the Lord is on me, because he has anointed me to preach good news to the poor. He has sent me to proclaim freedom for the prisoners and recovery of sight for the blind, to release the oppressed, to proclaim the year of the Lord's favor.*[5]

Good news! Healing for the broken-hearted! Freedom for the prisoners, sight for the blind, release for the oppressed, and the year of the Lord's favor! Through his church, Jesus continues to fulfill every promise of God to every generation. We proclaim the abolition of death and bring life and immortality to light *through the gospel!*[6] What a glorious gospel of peace, joy, abundant living, and hope![7]

What a power-filled message! Shout it from the housetops! Are you lost and alone on some forgotten highway? Our Father has provided a way back home! Do you feel separated from God? Jesus reconciles the Creator and the created! The only requirement is a spiritual transaction between God and man called faith!

Faith will come from hearing this message. It will not come through praying, miracles, great speakers, contemporary worship, beautiful buildings, or being good! God offers a contract with humanity. The life, death, burial and resurrection of Christ satisfy all the provisions of the contract absolutely without cost. All that remains is for mankind to accept the contract and receive its gracious benefits.

The acceptance process is *simplicity itself!* We humans must, of course, believe that the "party of the first part" exists and that Christ actually satisfies the conditions (and not our own merit). Then we agree to make the necessary change of direction (repentance) called for in the contract. We enter the contract and accept its benefits through our immersion into Christ. The Spirit of God takes up residence and past sins are forgiven...forgotten. Hope of glorious eternal life anoints hearts where only hopelessness dwelt before. At last! An anchor for our souls, moorings in the storms, light in the dark stormy trials and sufferings of life!

The blessings get better and better! Did you know that as we walk in the light and remain in the fellowship of God, the cleansing *continues?* Listen, you ain't heard nothin' yet! Our Father has designed a way, especially for us, assuring the very best of all possible lives.

For the *family*, a message of love between husband, wife and children reaches its most fulfilling level in Christ Jesus. Good tidings of agape see *any relationship* through the maze of thorns that rip, scratch, and threaten to tear it to pieces.

For the *estranged*, a message of reconciliation through Jesus on the cross — reunion and unity glued together by love.

For the *parent*, the discipline and instruction of the Lord Jesus provide a way of rearing loving, obedient, sensitive, compassionate, and responsible children.

For the *employer*, a management philosophy that creates and nurtures loyal, hardworking employees as Christ is seen at work in her life.

For the *employee*, the invigorating realization that he works for the Lord.

For the *businessperson*, a God-pleasing set of ethics and standards modeled on the Master and always profitable.

For the *professional*, a code of conduct derived from the life and inspiration of the Teacher insuring the conscientious and ethical pursuit of a career.

For the *politician,* the Lord's moral criterion excluding corruption and greed from public service and the governmental process.

For *governments*, a way of governing, given by the Prince of Peace, enabling men and women to live in harmony with others while assuring the best possible life for their citizens. As Leith Anderson puts it:

> Life is difficult and disappointing, and typical church-goers are struggling to survive. They come to church overflowing with needs - family, marriage, job, money, health, relationships — and looking for answers. They need hope and meaning and have turned to the church because they can't find it elsewhere.[8]

But are they finding it? If we are answering the questions people are asking, if we are focusing on matters that matter, if we are filled with the light of truth, if our lifestyles are different (or offer some difference) to the world's, if we are standing for the right among those who stand for nothing, then the answer is yes, yes in this life and yes for eternity!

The God who gave us life gave us *enlightenment.* The

deliverance of the ten commandments at Sinai lit the glowing candle of law. The coming of the Son of God bringing grace and truth into the world ignited the scintillating torch of glory.[9] What a message we have for those who dwell in darkness: *Dawn has broken!*

We have a great responsibility to present this message to the outsider in a palatable way. Our lives validate, lend credibility to, and adorn what we say. We gave some attention to these matters in theprevious chapter, but it needs reemphasis: we cannot separate the message from the medium.

Our *message* is the always perfect gospel. The *medium* is our imperfect selves. Both the treasure and its earthen container must be seen in an acceptable light. The gospel has the power to save. But it can only save when presented in an understandable way. Instead of "gospel" we can say, "good news". We can use "purity" for "sanctification", "rescue" for "salvation," "free gift" for "grace", "revealing" or "appearance" for "revelation." A gospel misunderstood is a gospel yet unpreached.

We Cannot Stop Speaking

Let me tell you a story of tragedy and triumph. It was a warm and sunny Sunday afternoon. The birds heralded the end of winter, and life for many was full of newness and hope...except for Ron Seward. To him, the sunshine was invisible. He was deaf to anything joyous such as the singing of birds. Trouble had entered his young life, and there seemed to be no solutions.

And so this handsome, accomplished, and popular youth put a revolver to his temple and pulled the trigger. He did this in spite of a lifetime of church attendance and righteous living in the home. Even though notes were left, the drastic nature of his last action remains a mystery.

Clouds of unspeakable pain overshadow the otherwise blessed and godly life of his surviving father, mother and siblings. Compounding the mourning that would ordinarily accompany the loss of a child are questions and self-incriminations borne of utter despair followed by periods of bleak and hopeless depression. Occasionally, the sun breaks through and a smile or laugh will make its escape.

The Sewards are Christians and they will survive, faith intact. To observers, they are victorious! Less than a year from that black Sunday, God began to use the event to reach precious souls. Several asked about their faith and the answer was always the same: "We have victory in Jesus." Since this catastrophe, the Sewards moved from the scene of tragedy to begin again in a new area. Already they are sowing seeds of the gospel in the hearts of the Welcome Wagon lady and the new hairdresser. *Nothing,* you see, can silence the child of God who understands the precious substance contained in the earthen vessel of his heart.

Peter and John found it impossible to keep silent even when threatened:

> *Then they called them in again and commanded them not to speak or teach at all in the name of Jesus. But Peter and John replied, "Judge for yourselves whether it is right in God's sight to obey you rather than God. For we cannot help speaking about what we have seen and heard..*[10]

Truly converted persons cannot bring themselves to *shut up!* You can tell them to, but they'll keep on doing and saying. The disciple of Jesus will *labor* and *suffer* for the gospel.

Not long ago, I delivered the funeral message for a man

named Bill Cullum. When I came to know Bill, he was suffering the effects of a stroke. Even though his face was a little distorted and his speech slurred, he always seemed to have a good attitude. Though it was often a struggle, especially for his loving wife, Bea, he was very regular in attendance

As I visited with Bea and their friends to gather some personal anecdotes for the funeral, they told about how a much younger Bill got fired for whistling. Bill was a man who habitually whistled while he worked. It was a subconscious expression of his cheerful, hardworking attitude. For some reason, his whistling began to irritate the owner of the plant nursery where he worked and she asked him to stop. He tried, but once again immersed in his work, the ol' lips puckered up and the whistling began again. Finally, the owner told him, "Bill, if you don't stop that whistling, I'm going to have to fire you!"

"Yes ma'am," said Bill with the best of intentions, "I'll stop right now." But, of course, he couldn't. It was too much a part of his personality. It was as natural as breathing. Sure enough, the sorehead owner fired Bill...for *whistling!*

Followers of Jesus are like that. Because Jesus is at the controls of their life, relating everything to him is as natural as puckering up was for Bill Cullum. When encountering problems, they automatically recall Jesus' words or actions in a similar circumstance. They naturally apply some principle or teaching from Jesus and the apostles. Like the whistling Bill Cullum, *they can't help it!*

One of my Bible instructors, Richard Rogers, used to say, "You can cut out their tongue and they'll learn sign language. If you cut off their arms, they'll learn how to tap out Morse Code with the stumps." The *only way* to stop Christians from speaking to others about the greatest thing that has ever happened to them is to murder them. Even then, as others have learned to their dismay, martyrdom may prolong and enhance the martyr's influence.

A Driving Faith

Christians speak because they feel *compelled.* They echo the apostle who said, *"For if I preach the gospel, I have nothing to boast of, for I am under compulsion; for woe is me if I do not preach the gospel."*[11] No one holds a gun to their heads. No one twists their arms. You see, we are not talking about external compulsion but internal combustion. *"According to what is written, 'I believed, therefore I spoke,' we also believe, therefore also we speak."*[12]

A faith that does not drive a person to testimony and witness is defective. Actually, is it proper to call it "faith" at all? Isn't this what James endeavors to get across in his letter?[13] Consequently, it is ludicrous to speak of regular attendees as "faithful." Faithfulness consists of more than legalistic responses to exhortations not to forsake the assembling.

It seems that every church has its compliment of "comatose Christians" as Ron Carlson puts it. These folks seem to sincerely have the idea that if they occupy their accustomed place every time the doors are open, they'll be able to do the same thing in that great auditorium in the sky.

Habitual attendance may fill a few pews that might otherwise be empty, but to what avail? Why don't we just buy some department store mannequins, dress them in Sunday-go-to-meetin' clothes and nail their bottoms to the pews? We'd have one of the best looking congregations money could buy! They might not give very much in the collection, or be able to sing and say "Amen," but they'd never *complain* either. In fact, they would never say *anything.* They would never have a message...they would never have a mission. They would never feel compelled to share their faith in word or deed because, you see, they are dead.

Habitual attenders are *spectators* at best. Write it down: Christianity is not a spectator sport! When *attenders* become *activists, dummies* become *doers,* the revolution will take off like a rocket!

I love the sign our evangelism committee put on the inside front doors of our building recently. As you leave the building, you read, "You are now entering the mission field." Yes! That's it! We are walking away from a time and place of *equipping* to a time of *using* that equipment to gospelize our world. We will encounter opportunities to do this in our homes, schools, and workplace if we *look* for them. The "mission field" is not a place we *go* but the place we *are!* We will feel our hearts inciting us to deliver the same transforming good news that has revolutionized our lives.

Several year ago, on the west flank of New Mexico's Sierra Blanca, I woke up on a cold October dawn. The previous night I inserted myself in my sleeping bag in the moonless darkness. Dazzled by a million points of ancient light filling my eyes, sleep was slow in coming. Now, looking to the West, the newly budding sun painted the golden red of autumn morning on tips of distant peaks. Silent in the still of morning, I watched the sunlight slide down the flanks of far mountains until it finally filtered through the pines surrounding our meadow and sprinkled me with glistening crystals of light.

How like the message of Christ! Born in beauty, it dissolves the darkness and its luminescent loveliness grows and becomes indescribably unique.

Perhaps the same thought occurred to John Keble as he exulted, "Sun of my soul! Thou Saviour dear, It is not night if Thou be near."[14] Bernard of Clairvaux reflected,

Jesus, thou Joy of loving hearts!
Thou fount of life! Thou light of men!

From the best bliss that earth imparts,
We turn...unfilled...to thee again.

Spoken by prophets, sung by angels, revealed by the Son of God...*what a message!*

[1] Formerly *Sunset School of Preaching*

[2] Mike Armour, from a taped sermon, *"Rethinking Evangelism"* delivered at Skillman Avenue Church of Christ, 10/18/92

[3] Elton Trueblood, *The Company of the Committed,* Harper & Row, publishers, New York, 1961, p. 45

[4]Romans 8:35-39
[5]Luke 4:18,19
[6]2 Timothy 1:10
[7]Ephesians 6:5; 2 Corinthians 4:3,4; 1 Timothy 1:11
[8]Leith Anderson, *Dying for Change*, p. 17
[9]John 1:17
[10]Acts 4:18-20
[11]I Corinthians 9:16 (NASB)
[12]2 Corinthians 4:13 (NASB)
[13]James 2:18-26
[14]Hymn by John Keble

7

WAR

He was not aiming, he was just shooting. He held the rifle over his head and kept the trigger down, pumping round after round into the jungle at an unseen enemy. He knew they were out there, all around, blending in the shadows. He saw their bullets take the lives of the two young men in front of him. Panic stricken, he called in air strikes. He called for reinforcements, he called for rescue choppers. It was Vietnam, it was horrifying, and it was in our living rooms on television .

Vietnam was a blatant, "in your face" war because brave cameramen and foolhardy reporters put it there. As we watched the fighting that filled the body bags it was impossible to deny we were at war. Thousands of young men and women made one-way trips to the steaming jungles of Vietnam. Those who run their fingers along the names etched into the Vietnam war memorial find it impossible to avoid tears in the eyes and lumps in the throat.

On a spiritual plane, Christians struggle for life and death in battles just as real. In the New Testament, words such as *warfare, soldiers, weapons, armor, conquer,* and other military figures march across the pages. Writers and poets recruit militant themes for Christian music, poetry and prose with great enthusiasm. We think we understand war. But I wonder, do we really understand?

Our perceptions of war and actual vile, muddy, exhausting, terrifying, reality are poles apart. The difference between cushioned congregations singing, *"Onward Christian Soldiers"* and the hardship, dust and blood of a *real* army reports how far we have drifted from the New Testament ideal.

True soldiers don't have the luxury to decide where and when they will go into battle. In the church of today, we come and go as we like. We give of our time and money as we see fit. We serve when convenient...if we get around to it. They'd laugh you out of the sanctuary if you suggested sending members on missions they could not refuse. Give someone a job and hold them accountable for it? Not likely!

You know, I can't recall hearing anyone referred to as a "fellow soldier" these days. We appear as different from a real army as chalk and cheese.

The idea of church as army was not strange to early Christians. Notice the military language in passages such as these: *"Ephaphroditus my brother and fellow soldier..."*[1] *"Suffer hardship with me as a good soldier of Christ Jesus..."*[2] *"Archippus our fellow soldier..."* [3]*"Put on the full armor of God..."* [4]. Soldiers fight in armies. Armies fight in wars. If we are soldiers in an army, then we must be at war!

The Nature of Our Warfare

No true Christian ever shed another's blood or physically killed anyone in the name of Jesus Christ. Genuine, authentic Christians don't fight that way. According to the Holy Spirit, we are locked in *spiritual* warfare. Carefully read these inspired passages:

For though we live in the world, we do

*not wage war as the world does. The
weapons we fight with are not the
weapons of the world. On the contrary,
they have divine power to demolish
strongholds. We demolish arguments
and every pretension that sets itself up
against the knowledge of God, and we
take captive every thought to make it
obedient to Christ.*[5]

*Put on the full armor of God so that you
can take your stand against the devil's
schemes. For our struggle is not
against flesh and blood, but against the
rulers, against the authorities, against
the powers of this dark world and
against the spiritual forces of evil in the
heavenly realms. Therefore put on the
full armor of God.* [6]

Our warfare should not consist of people crowding into
an auditorium to provide an audience for a speaker! Passive
observance of rituals over and over fifty-two times a year isn't
war! War means *fighting,* driving back an opposing armed
force, conquering territory, and liberating populations by
reaching out to them with powerful, life-changing answers.

Though we have allowed distractions to divert us and
bog us down in the mud of complacency, the objectives remain
the same: destruction of the strongholds of Satan, demolishing
the artillery of arguments and pretentious missiles aimed at the
knowledge of God, and taking thoughts captive to the obedience to Christ.

Our mission and Paul's are identical: *"To open their
eyes and turn them from darkness to light, and from the power
of Satan to God, so that they may receive forgiveness of sins
and a place among those who are sanctified by faith in me."*

(Acts 26:17,18) False religions, godless humanistic philosophies, and New Age mumbo-jumbo presently have free course in this world. Lofty, pretensions and high-sounding, but empty speculations capture hearts and minds of people. Unless people accidentally stumble into a church building on Sunday morning, they will hear nothing else.

When Jude said to *contend for the faith*,[7] he was not urging a *defensive* posture. To contend for any cause involves taking the *offensive*. It means accepting responsibility to fight for the promotion and defense of the faith. Have we obediently responded to this inspired command? When Paul charged the Ephesians to expose the deeds of darkness by shining the light of truth on them,[8] what did he expect?

The Light Brigade

If you're like me, you find angry shouting on street corners by sign-carrying self-styled "fundamentalists" a real turn-off. Personally, I have no intention of being lumped together with what I consider to be a zit on the face of Christianity. So, if the only alternative means acting like them, *count me out.* I'd rather do *nothing at all!*

Of course, "nothing at all," is not an option for a disciple of Jesus Christ. He chose to *do something* and, since I follow Him, I too will choose to do something. Our warfare must take the same shape as that of Jesus, the apostles, and the early church. We must assume the same role in society, culture and community. We will be no more liked, tolerated or included than the shouting sign-wavers, but we will be *right.*

Satan is practicing germ warfare! As spreads his filthy spawn, epidemics of social sickness infect Western culture. Widely accepted speculations and arguments spew from carriers of the devil's diseases. Immorality, idolatry (as in the form of materialism), corruption, and atheistic humanism continue to plague human society. To apply the medicine of God's truth to these diseases is to imitate the Great Physician. His strategy? Confront diseases not symptoms. The apostles did not defy the works of Satan, but Satan himself. The deeds of flesh and darkness wage war against our souls.9 But, as Paul points out in the Ephesians passage, we smash these by exposing them to the light. We are "The Light Brigade!"

What a true and great old saying: *Better to light a candle than to curse the darkness*! Being children of light,10 we must be in positions to light the candle of truth where darkness lurks. Instead of shouting down the pagans who do wrong, a revolution will occur when we *do* right regardless of cost or consequence. A Christian serving on a school board, for example, can influence others to legislate Christian morals and ethics. Name calling, mudslinging, throwing tantrums and little fits at meetings and hearings is like a faceful of bad breath.

Here's an excellent example: vocal, humanistic minorities (often consisting of one person) backed by the ACLU, drive many school districts' policies. Recently *one student*, his family, and the ACLU completely eliminated prayer from one school in a district close to my home. As polls and surveys invariably prove, such a policy did not reflect the will of the vast majority of my neighbors.

My public high school not only taught Judeo-Christian values, but broadcast prayer over the public address system as each school day began. Classes consisted of mostly religious students, a sprinkling of atheists, agnostics, and of course, renegades. No one expected the non-religious contingent to participate in prayer, so they didn't. Today they would likely contact the ACLU and spend multiplied thousands of taxpayer dollars to insure that if they don't want to pray, *no one else gets to!*

It is time to stand up and make a difference! We must

take back our streets, neighborhoods, shopping centers, and schools. How? By attending meetings, writing letters and articles, public speaking, running for office or otherwise becoming active; bringing light to darkness!. Besides being our right and privilege in most Western nations, we have an obligation as disciples of Christ. Schools and other organizations listen to those who speak up, not those who roll over, go to sleep, or play dead.

I know people who refuse to watch the news on television because of all the violence, immorality and crime. Radical, *revolutionary* Christians, however, will realize that evil does not go away because we ignore it. Pretending it doesn't exist only allows matters to grow worse. We must have the guts to fight Satan on his own turf. That means rushing into the dark, dank rooms of our culture, throwing open the windows. The light of truth will flood in. The fresh air of righteousness will blow in. That's what Jesus did. That's what *we* must do.

Never Underestimate the Enemy

Shortly before dawn, an old king awakens with a start. Cold sweat coats his clammy face. His heart beats wildly. He realizes he's been dreaming again, but the old, familiar waves of fear continue to wash over him even in consciousness. He remembers dreaming about successful spring campaigns, especially battles with Philistines, their giants, and their iron weapons. He tries hard to remember the rest of the exploded dream but the remaining fragments drift away in the dawn. The residue of the nightmare remains as a gnawing question throbbing in his aching head. Satan, the father of lies, has implanted doubt in his brain. The master of deception has sown fear into the heart of one with no reason to fear. *How big is my army, really? Do I have enough men to defend us?* He calls for Joab.

Joab stands in the presence of his king, eyes downcast, not believing what he is hearing. "Go and count the Israelites from Beersheba to Dan. Then report back to me," David says, "so that I may know how many there are."

"May the Lord multiply his troops a hundred times over," replies Joab. "My lord the king, are they not all my lord's subjects? Why does my lord want to do this? Why should he bring guilt on Israel?"[11]

Read the book of 1st Chronicles for the rest of the story. David insisted on the unlawful census and 70,000 people perished. Why? Because he listened to Satan.

Yes, the enemy is Satan.

> *And the great dragon was thrown down, the serpent of old who is called the devil and Satan, who deceives the whole world; he was thrown down to the earth, and his angels were thrown down with him.* [12]

Havelock Ellis was right when he observed, "A religion can no more afford to degrade its devil than to degrade its God." Satan is *real*, real as Father, Son and Holy Spirit. He's as real as the angels (used to be one, apparently). Yet, belief in Satan declines. In a 1974 Harris poll, 53% of Americans believed in his existence. By 1980, according to a Gallup poll, that group had declined to 34%. Today, according to the Barna Research Group, three out of five do not believe Satan exists.[13]

Satan has to have permission to seek our destruction. Once he has it, the old saying applies: *All's fair in love and war.* He uses both people and nature to kill and destroy. Thus, Jesus warned Peter, *"Simon, Simon, Satan has asked to sift you as wheat. But I have prayed for you, Simon, that your faith may not fail. And when you have turned back, strengthen your brothers.*"[14] Satan was going to "sift" Peter, but his goal was Peter's destruction. And so Peter warns us,

> *Be self-controlled and alert. Your enemy the devil prowls around like a roaring lion looking for someone to devour. Resist him, standing firm in the faith, because you know that your brothers throughout the world are undergoing the same kind of sufferings.*[15]

Can Satan *still* demand and receive permission to sift us? Is it possible, sifter in hand, he's sifting you and/or yours right now?

Job learned a great deal about spiritual warfare when Satan received permission to test the integrity of his faith. Yahweh allowed Satan to take away everything that was precious to Job except his life. As he surveyed the scarred and cratered battlefield of his world, devoid of any reason to believe, Job did the only thing spiritual survivors *can do.* He stubbornly clung to his faith with no visible means of support. Satan lost that battle because Job *stood,* firmly defending his position. When we resist the hound of hell, he slinks away, tail between his legs, *defeated!*[16]

One of the most clever tricks ever played by Satan is getting us to think of him as a funny fairy in red tights, with horns, hoofs, tail, pitchfork, and evil leer. You can forget that! As Shakespeare wrote in King Lear, Act III, "The prince of darkness is a gentleman." If he ever takes physical form it will be subtly done. He's not going to introduce himself and hand you a card:

SATAN & ASSOCIATES

Lucifer Beelzebub, Prop.

Deception, Lies, Discouragement, Confusion, Distraction
Experts in Evil and Destruction
Headquarters: Lake of Fire Rd., Gehenna

Phone: 1-800-666-HELL

Most likely, his card would look more like this:

THE REVEREND

G.I. Feelgood

Happiness, Pleasure, Wealth, Status,
Physical Fitness.
Hedonism without guilt a specialty.
1001 Broad Way, New Age
1-800 FIX-U-UPP

*"For even Satan disguises himself as an angel of light.
Therefore it is not surprising if his servants also disguise themselves as servants of righteousness."*[17]   Satan, Pied Piper of
Gehenna, pipes a merry, seductive tune leading us astray from
purity and devotion to Christ.[18]   We are unwary children, distracted, unfocused, and deceived!

Let us shake off deception and focus on the important.
Satan has no power over us that we don't furnish him, free for
the taking. Enough is enough! Now, put on the full armor of
God and *stand!*

The Battleground

The arena is the heavenly places[19] but the battleground is the world. Jesus saw death approaching and mused, *"Now is the time for judgment on this world; now the prince of this world will be driven out."*[20] Paul warned the Corinthians, *"The God of this world has blinded the minds of the unbelieving, that they might not see the light of the gospel of the glory of Christ, who is the image of God."*[21] John addresses the Christian's protection and the world's predicament as he writes, *"He who was born of God keeps (us) and the evil one does not touch him. We know that we are of God, and the whole world lies in the power of the evil one."*[22]

For proof of Satan's control of the world, just observe current events. As Don Carragher has written:

> The airwaves have become a platform for anti-Christian messages and a home-study academy whose consistent lecture in our living rooms is: "If it feels good, it's OK." Our judicial system argues about shades of guilt, blurring the distinction between right and wrong until it becomes all but invisible...a system in which the guilty are set free and the innocent punished. Our government now unleashes heavily armed para-military units to attack religious groups which are deemed to be a "threat to the peace", while at the same time, criminal gangs roam our streets virtually unmolested - killing, maiming and raping. Parents murder their children, children murder their parents for inheritance, madmen eat the remains of their murdered victims. Children are abducted, sexually tortured and killed. Drugs and drug-related crimes rampage every facet

> of our society. Drivers kill other drivers
> in traffic jams or, for no seeming reason
> whatever...Killers enter play grounds
> and spray bullets into little children
> because they themselves had an "unhap-
> py childhood". Homosexuality is con-
> doned and taught about in our schools,
> treated as a "freedom". If all this does-
> n't frighten us, it's a sure sign that Satan
> has clouded our eyes and dulled...moral-
> ity to this madness he has created in our
> world. He's injecting the narcotic of
> acceptance into our souls![23]

A revolution will occur when the army of light
becomes eager for the fight! When we actually *seek* positions
to struggle against the domain of darkness, we'll see some
action! Our youth, for example, will seek certain professions
not just to survive and prosper, but to reflect the light of righteousness.

Christians will take inventory of talents and abilities
then seek positions and opportunities to inflict the greatest possible damage on the enemy. They will endeavor to become
teachers, reporters, publishers, makers of motion pictures,
writers, preachers, shapers of public opinion. They will engage
the enemy in furious combat for the hearts and minds of men,
women and children. Carragher writes,

> Let us become the 300 Spartans, who,
> when the Greek city-states were unable
> to agree on how to deal with the threat-
> ening Persian army, went alone to the
> pass and held off for weeks the mighti-
> est army the world had ever seen. Yes,
> the 300 Spartans died in that pass, but
> in performing their mighty deed, they
> inspired the entire Greek nation to rise

up and defeat the Persians.[24]

Listen! Can you hear the trumpet? Let the soldiers of Christ counter-attack the dark army in the mountain passes of the media, on the plains of our educational systems, on the beaches of our social services, in the streets of our law-enforcement agencies! Christian attorneys and judges can battle in the jungles of our judicial systems. Christian men and women can pursue public office to seek and destroy Satan's entrenched forces on our councils, parliaments, and legislatures.

The Battle for the Holy Hill

Among the most blood-stained fields of battle is the church. In every generation, Satan infiltrates the church donning various disguises. Paul warned the Ephesian elders of *"savage wolves"* that *"from your own number"* would ravage the flock seeking to draw away disciples.[25]

Since Satan's success depends upon our ignorance, complacency, and lethargy, warnings against the multiple forms of his treachery pack New Testament letters . His victory becomes evident in every self-absorbed, inward-turned, self-satisfied and self-destructing church in the world.

We challenge what we *can't* see by confronting what we *can*. For example, using the word, we can scan for false teachers and false doctrines (*true* error, not speculations or opinions). We can insist our teachers and preachers have a clear "this is what the Lord says" for everything they teach. We must gently instruct those who recklessly oppose the truth, attempting to rescue them from the devil's ambush.[26]

False doctrine is not the only enemy in our pulpits and classrooms. We are surrounded by unwitting accomplices who use *no doctrine at all!* It should disturb us to hear of entire quarters spent reading someone's pop psychology book. Unless books constantly and continually seek to help us understand and apply God's word, they don't belong in a Bible class.

We are withering spiritually for lack of even basic Bible knowledge. Skeptical? Just make up a simple anonymous questionnaire (no one signs their name). Ask very basic questions about the Bible and a few "first principles." Your skepticism will vanish as you realize the tremendous ignorance that exists. So many are not equipped to take the offense because they are *defenseless!* Battle-ready soldiers must be *in the word.* When we get there and bring others with us, the world will explode with awesome revolution of a magnitude never before witnessed.

Diotrephes and His Kin

He goes by the name of Diotrephes,[27] but you may know his modern counterpart as Sam, Fred, Walter, or some other name. He may be the "chief elder" or other local "synagogue demagogue" who decides what is best for everyone else. He rules with sheer force of personality. He wont step down or relinquish his position because he "loves to be first."

A friend of mine knew he was in trouble one place he preached when one of the elders told him, "When it comes to making decisions, we all just defer to the wisdom of old brother D." Over the next few years, he watched Brother D. run the show. Sure enough, the others deferred to him, *right or wrong.* I didn't ask Satan personally, but I'm sure he *loved* it!

The *Diotrephes Syndrome*, however, takes many forms...the most common being the "squeaky-wheel". Many churches are "blessed" with these well-meaning but misguided obstructionists" who are against everything and for nothing. Characterizing themselves as "concerned" and "wishing only the best for the Lord's church," they are the complainers, the

whiners, the high-maintenance nay-sayers who make life difficult for everyone else. They may be sincere but they are tuned-
in to the wrong channel. If they gain the ear of the leadership,
they do great damage.

Certain code-words and phrases identify these unwitting allies of Satan. For example, they usually begin their
complaints something like this: *"Many people think* (this or
that) and *I heard several say* that *they are going to leave* if (this
or that) is (done or not done)."* We make a mistake if we think
"many people" actually means many people. It really means
"Me and the other two or three soreheads I hang with." If we
consistently ignore them, then the proverb applies: *"For lack
of wood the fire goes out, and where there is no whisperer, con-
tention quiets down. Like charcoal to hot embers and wood to
fire, So is a contentious man to kindle strife."*[28]

The most devastating ploy of the devil pits us against
each other. We waste our time and energies fighting with our
brothers and sisters. As a kid, I got spankings for such imma-
ture behavior! Paul asked the Corinthians a sobering question,
*"For since there is jealousy and quarreling among you, are
you not worldly? Are you not acting like mere men?"*[29]

We invite Satan to establish beachheads in our churches and homes by treating each other as adversaries. *"Do not
let the sun go down while you are still angry,"* writes Paul,
"and do not give the devil a foothold."[30] Our problem is ignorance, ignorance of the war raging around us, and ignorance of
Satan's schemes.[31]

We haven't identified the enemy! When he tricks us
into seeing *each other* as the enemy he wins by default. The
Holy Spirit warns us of the consequences through Paul:

> *"For I am afraid that when I come I
> may not find you as I want you to be,
> and you may not find me as you want me*

to be. I fear that there may be quarrel-
ing, jealousy, outbursts of anger, fac-
tions, slander, gossip, arrogance and
disorder."[32]

The army of God cannot afford infighting because armies that turn upon themselves self-destruct.

The Victory

Christians observe those in the world and become confused by how "easy" they have it. Look more closely. Satan obviously has them under control. Centuries ago, Thomas A Kempis said, "The devil does not tempt unbelievers and sinners who are already his own."[33] Their *will* already belongs to him! The human *will* is the prize of war. David's satanic inspiration to number Israel provides a case in point. Wiersbe writes,

Satan's goal is always to get to the will
and control it. He may begin by deceiv-
ing the mind, as with Eve, or by attacking the body, as with Job; but ultimately
he must get to the will. However, in
David's case, Satan bypassed the mind
and the body and in a blitzkrieg action
attacked his will and won.[34]

When Satan filled the heart of Ananias to lie, he attacked and conquered his *will.*[35] As Mr. Wiersbe has observed, "The Christian life is basically a matter of the will."[36] This basic, motivating factor called the *will* is up for grabs in war with the dark lord.

The news for Christian soldiers, however, has never been better. We are *more* than conquerors.[37] How many contests have you heard of where you can win by just *fighting?* Someone once observed, "The only thing necessary for evil to triumph is for good men to do nothing." Christians must keep in mind, however, that "The only thing necessary for righteousness to triumph is for good men to do something."

Wherever, whenever saints of light march into the kingdom of darkness, Satan beats a hasty retreat. Victory, you see, is guaranteed! James reveals a no-fail tactic: *"Submit yourselves, then, to God. Resist the devil, and he will flee from you."[38]*

The question remains, however: who flees from whom? Will we be confident and resolute, or shrink back to destruction?[39] Flight becomes a valid tactic when handling temptation (Joseph dealing with Potiphar's wife, for example), but we must not quit the battlefield in cowardly retreat just because the going gets tough. As A Kempis said so long ago, "By flight alone we cannot conquer; but by patience and true humility we become stronger than all our enemies."[40]

Christian soldiers grow stronger because God's unconquerable Holy Spirit controls the patient and humble. And, as John assures us, *"You, dear children, are from God and have overcome them, because the one who is in you is greater than the one who is in the world."[41]* The mere knowledge of the presence of God's Spirit fills us with bravado that only an armored, armed, and confident soldier can have. Can we win? Yes, if we will **fight**, *"The God of peace will soon crush Satan under your feet."[42]*

Saigon, April 30, 1975

The shameful image is burned into our consciousness: one helicopter after another touching down on the roof of the American embassy, instantly crammed with panic-stricken refugees. The final, frenzied evacuation from Saigon is underway. People are crying, pushing, shoving trying to get on the next chopper, and clinging to the landing gear as the Vietcong roll triumphantly into the city. Peace with honor? Hardly!

In Vietnam now, the jungles are quiet. In the fields, farmers plant rice around the bomb craters. Tourists, many of them former soldiers, tour the areas where they lost their youth in frustrating, fruitless battle. For the most part, Communism has crumbled, without war, under the weight of its own corruption. But honest history books will recount how soldiers in black pajamas, wearing sandals made of discarded tires; defeated the United States and their allies. They will tell how their northern sponsors endured thousands of tons of bombs, naval shelling, air strikes and napalm but kept on coming.

How could such a thing happen to the most powerful alliance on the face of the earth? Apart from the fact that we should not have been there at all, we did not know our enemy. We were ignorant of his schemes. American and Australian forces, led by the inept and hesitant, simply could not resist the Viet Cong and North Vietnamese resolve to fight, whatever the cost, to the bitter end.

Rwanda, April 1994

We look at the pictures and it seems unbelievable. Rotting human corpses pave the roads and choke the rivers and lakes. Unarmed men, women and children of one tribe hacked to death with machetes by another, simply for existing. One observer commented that hell had been emptied of its devils — they were all in Rwanda.

Perhaps the observer is right because that's how Satan fights. The children of light are legitimate targets simply because we exist. Satan seeks to destroy us whether we fight back or not. Unlike the unarmed Rwandans, we have access to both arms and armor. And yet, sword and armor laid aside, oblivious to the war itself, Christians are hacked to spiritual death.

When will we ever learn?
The answer, my friend, is blowin' in the wind.

[1]Philippians 2:25
[2]2 Timothy 2:3 (NASB)
[3]Philemon 2
[4]Ephesians 6:11
[5]2 Corinthians 10:3,4
[6] Ephesians 6:11-13
[7]Jude 3
[8]Ephesians 5:8-13
[9]Ephesians 5:3-14; Galatians 5:16-23
[10]1 Thessalonians 5:5
[11]1 Chronicles 21:1-3
[12]Revelation 12:9 New American Standard Bible
[13]George Barna, *Absolute Confusion*, Regal Books, a division of Gospel Light, Ventura, CA 93006, 1993, p. 139

[14]Luke 22:31
[15]1Peter 5:8,9
[16]James 4:7
[17]2 Corinthians 11:14,15 (NASB)
[18]2 Corinthians 11:3
[19]Ephesians 6:12
[20]John 12:31
[21]2 Corinthians 4:4 (NASB)
[22]1 John 5:18,19 (NASB)
[23]Donald Carragher, unpublished paper, "Under Siege", Grapevine Texas, May, 1994
[24]Don Carragher, "Under Siege."
[25]Acts 20:29,30
[26]2 Timothy 2:25,26
[27]3 John 9,10
[28]Prov. 26:20,21 (NASB)
[29]1 Corinthians 3:3
[30]Ephesians 4:26,27
[31]2 Corinthians 2:11
[32]2 Corinthians 12:20
[33]Thomas A Kempis, *Of the Imitation of Christ*, London: Burns and Oates, 1908, p.
[34]Warren W. Wiersbe, *The Strategy of Satan,* Tyndale House Publishers, Inc., Wheaton, Illinois, 1981, page 61.
[35]Acts 5:3
[36]Warren Wiersbe, p. 62
[37]Romans 8:37
[38]James 4:7
[39]Hebrews 10:35-39
[40]Thomas A Kempis, p. 22
[41]1 John 4:4
[42]Romans 16:20

8

MONKEY WRENCHES

The Story of Mike's Church

Continual difficulty plagued the Central Church where Mike attended. On the surface, all was well: an affluent group of people in a comfortable suburban church building; enjoying the good will and respect of the community. Penetrate the thin skin of respectability, though, and things were different. Attendance had been the same for years. "Just the right size," thought Mike. "I know everyone and everyone knows me." At the same time, he felt a gnawing inside. He knew the Central church was not well.

He could remember an exciting time of newness and growth when they met in the local school. Planning began for a building. Sacrificial gifts for the building reflected enthusiasm and optimism. They were thrilled about a missionary family they helped support in Thailand. Their enthusiastic preacher was fired-up and positive. Thankful celebration filled their times of worship.

Now, only five years later, fiery enthusiasm had cooled to icy apathy. The sermons became irrelevant and negative, more applicable to *someone* else *somewhere* else. Rumblings of discontent and gossip hung about like threatening storms. Attendance "plateaued." Contributions barely covered expenses. Perpetual rumors circulated of tension between staff and church leaders. Baptisms were rare. The church had recently recalled one of the foreign missionaries due to lack of funds.

Mike knew he should be more involved in the life of the church, reaching out to others, seeking opportunities for good works, and inviting people to attend. He just felt unable, under the circumstances, to work up any enthusiasm. Slowly, he descended to the level of a mere auditor, an unmotivated, uninvolved spectator. He knew the majority of folks felt the same as he did. What he didn't know was, in the unseen spiritual dimension, a battle had been lost. There, the latest entry on the last page of Satan's Book of Victories, proudly listed the decline and fall of the Central Church. In Heaven, the angel who recorded casualties and lost territory could barely see through the tears to make the entry: "Central Church, killed by apathy."

Satan loves to throw monkey wrenches in the works! We can count on him trying to sabotage every good work. Recently, the church has been as much of a threat to the devil as a mosquito making menacing circles around an elephant. Unopposed and unhindered, he works to turn the church from a hostile army into an unwitting ally. In our present form, we pose no real threat to his subversive work of distraction and neutralization. Who's afraid of an army that believes fighting consists of getting into groups and holding weekly pep talks?

Our invisible, inoffensive, and non-invasive Christianity provides puny competition for Satan and his growing control of the media and legal establishment. We make little impact on the secular educational systems of our present culture. Our recent contributions to higher moral standards and ethics cause no more ripples than feathers coming to rest on the surface of a serene pond.

We have instead spent our energies in the creation of impressive brick and stone monuments. Institutions of higher learning have become the focus of attention. Any impact we may have upon the morality of our world goes mostly unnoticed and unsung. How *tragic!* Christian men and women should rise as cream to the top of our democratic institutions. Instead, many of these institutions rot from the inside out with self-serving greed. Choking on the stale air of corruption, a slowly suffocating society cries out for Christianity's fresh breeze.

Where are the Christian judges, representatives, senators, prime ministers, governors, premiers and presidents renowned for standards of justice and righteousness glorifying God while elevating the nations?

Obviously, leavening our culture with the yeast of Christian principles is on hold. Confronting the devil and those in his grasp lies far to the back our idle Christian minds. On the other hand, Satan, diabolically successful, "works like the devil." Remember that old saying about the devil and idle minds? Unnoticed and therefore unopposed, he tosses monkey wrenches into just the right places to bring the kingdom's machinery to a grinding halt.

Satan does his work in a subtle and crafty manner few are able to detect.[1] This Master of Deception, excels at disguising a hindrance as a help. Every time we detect and destroy one of his ploys, he resurfaces with a new one. Our best defense remains an educated offense.[2] Together, we will consider just a few of his successful strategies.

Flocks With Blind Shepherds

Blindness means the absence of vision. Shepherds

with no vision have no idea where they're going, much less where to lead the flock. Along with applying the qualifications listed in Paul's letters to Timothy and Titus, churches should ask prospective shepherds, "Tell us your vision for this church and the cause of Christ." and, "How do you propose to lead us toward your vision?" Men without vision are simply not qualified to oversee the church.

Paul, speaking to the Ephesian elders as recorded in Acts 20, could not have made it any clearer. The *Holy Spirit* appoints elders. When we ordain elders, we simply recognize the work of the Spirit. But how can mere mortals tell whom the Holy Spirit appoints? Again, refer to the list in 1 Timothy and Titus. Furthermore, does he have a flock? If he has no flock (disciples who look to him as spiritual leader), he must not yet be ready to serve as a shepherd. Simple!

No congregation rises above its leaders. Churches under leadership of misled pastors blind to the needs of the world offer special challenges. Some leaders, prematurely appointed, are blind because of scriptural ignorance.

Blind ignorance in a humble person lasts only as long as it takes to open his eyes to the light. However, when this blindness results from *willful* ignorance, we have major problems. If it results from *pride* or *arrogance,* Satan has a foothold. It may become necessary to go to the proverbial "plan B."

"Plan B" consists of doing what you *know* to be right with or *without* leadership. In this plan, *you* become the leader. Suffering in various forms comes to the disciple going against the wishes of a blind leadership...so what's new? Become involved in your community. Seek to influence the decision-making bodies in your school district, county, city, township, parish, state and nation. Teach, immerse, hold Bible studies, lead devotionals and pray with those you reach. If dull, listless worship experiences are dragging you, or someone you convert down, counter this with additional celebrative and edifying times of worship in your home.

If you insist on practicing visible, influential, and evangelistic discipleship, the leadership may drive you out anyway (sad to say, I have witnessed such a travesty myself). This result, of course, lies beyond your control provided your behavior has been righteous. Keeping a clear conscience by *never* being willfully divisive remains *vital*.

Membership, even in a dull, negative and invisible group, remains valuable for one simple reason. As long as you are a part of it, you exert an influence for radical, positive, scriptural, change. Leave and your influence leaves with you.

Some leaders have the idea "overseer" means "boss." But "looking out over" the flock is not the work of dictators. Closed-door meetings where "official policies" are decided do not express concern for the sheep. Elders who would "lord it over" the flock of God concerned Peter enough to issue the warning recorded in 1 Peter 5:1-4. This passage ought begin every meeting of church leaders. Jim Bill McInteer opined,

> "Across this land I pray with my brethren in public assembly. One petition I notice repetitiously...is this: "Lord, bless our elders and help them make wise decisions!" Somehow it leaves me cold..."help them make decisions." Is that their job? I want an elder, not a board. I want a Godly, praying, thoughtful, sensitive man. I want one to come to me when I'm weak, sick, strong, successful, bewildered. I want a precious leader in Christ that shares his greater strength with me. "Help them make the right decisions?" Really. I want a brother who helps make me right in the holy sight of God. That's my

prayer!

Jesus Christ supersedes all leaders. He plunged into the troubled waters of his world. He wove his way into the fabric of the Jewish nation to challenge the very fibers of it. He made a large circle of friends among the sinners. He associated with the outcasts of his day. He had dinner with them. He stood toe-to-toe with the ancient counterparts of corrupt and self-serving politicians. He was accessible and visible. He was influential because he was on the offensive. As he looked upon the multitudes, he felt a compassion of such strength that cloistering himself in cool, cushioned comfort was unthinkable. The world around him was in danger of eternal fire. He would not stop until his blood quenched it. He is *the* Good Shepherd. All true shepherds of the flock will, *with eyes wide open,* pastor the flock over which the Holy Spirit has made them overseers.[3]

Laws, Rules, and Traditions

Some argue loud and long for freedom in Christ, but they really want "religious entitlement" or an *absence of definite rules.* Here's how the argument runs: *since we are no longer under law, rules no longer apply.* This primarily seeks to justify attitudes, lifestyles and practices in the absence of scriptural authority. Frequently, it attempts to justify the addition of anti-scriptural innovations for which no firm biblical authority or basis exists.

While freedom very definitely resides in him, this does not license us to serve the flesh (our own interests and pleasures).[4] One of the fastest growing churches in Japan provides an example of the "no rules" doctrine gone to seed. The Perfect Liberty Church is a group where anything goes. You can do whatever you deem necessary to achieve "perfect fulfillment." The church owns a complete recreation facility where you can do exactly what you want from praying or playing golf to getting involved in group sex. Excuse me...I thought we were serving God, not ourselves.

Does the fact we are not under law but grace mean no rules now apply to the work and worship of Christians? Or, as Paul puts it, "What then? Shall we sin because we are not under law but under grace? By no means!"[5]

In Romans, Galatians, and Hebrews, the Holy Spirit says there can be no justification by the legal system of the Law of Moses or *any other law*.[6] The covenant of Sinai now stands obsolete as a means of *justification*.[7] By *justification*, we mean forgiveness of sins that restores our fellowship with God. No *law* can do what Jesus has already done on the cross.

On the other hand, *rules*, such as those for worship and daily conduct, are not useless legalistic remnants of bygone days. They are necessary regulators of our individual and collective work. They guide our worship under a new covenant. They are the means of smooth and efficient order as we function in the assembly of the church. F. LaGard Smith has written,

> Proper church organization and function does not in itself get us 'right' with God. But improper church organization and function (whether because of sterile tradition or un-biblical innovation) may indeed get us "wrong" with God.[8]

We live and work for the progress of the gospel, the spread of the kingdom. As we assemble on the first day of the week,[9] we sing, eat bread, and sip wine. We fulfill the purpose of glorifying God. We edify and encourage one another as we worship. The rules apply — not to justify us, but to please God. These principles are the means God has chosen to unify us. This is how he equips us to fulfill our destiny.

God did not give us rules to suppress spontaneity and expression. On the contrary, rules help *facilitate* them. No one is left out. Everyone is built up. *Suppression* apparently becomes the goal, however, of some who forbid exclamations of praise and agreement (Hallelujah! Amen!). Some forbid harmless, natural expressions of joy and approval, such as applause. Others argue against selected individuals or groups singing in the church as if this violated some scripture. This position totally relies on constant appeals to Greek verbs and their tenses.[10] It is a shaky position at best. The mental gymnastics required by such flimsy and forced logic make it unworthy of serious consideration.

Scriptural, to some folks, means "the way we've always done it." We conveniently overlook the inheritance of some of our "ways" from the Roman Catholic Church and other religious groups. Many practices are simply time-honored traditions, but hardly apostolic in origin. So much of what we do traditionally is simply *customary,*[11] left-overs from another time when they were relevant. They easily become irrelevant hindrances to communicating the gospel and edifying the saints.

When it comes to concepts and perspectives, changing gears becomes very difficult. As we get older, accepting new ways of doing things...new thoughts...new truths gets even *more* difficult. And yet, progress makes it *necessary.* It comes as no secret Christianity can be both *comfortable* and *uncomfortable.* Comfortable because Jesus always remains the same.[12] Comfortable because God's requirements and rewards never change. This rock-solid *unchangeableness* provides us a great deal of security in an uncertain age.

Christianity can become *uncomfortable* when we realize much of the *practice* of it is completely flexible. For those who love predictable routine, the very idea that Christians can relate to our world in highly varied and unpredictable ways disconcerts them. For example, we have not made sufficient use of the arts, such as music and drama. We have failed to snap-up opportunities opened by cable television.

The fact remains Christians must look at their world asking themselves, "Is there a better way to do this? Are there other things I can do to reach my neighbors with the gospel, things that do not violate scripture?" God's word offers tremendous latitude in the matter of *how* we preach the gospel. One thing for sure, *what we are doing now fails to reach our planet.* We must have bold, drastic, and innovative changes. We must have them *urgently!*

We must stop seeing ourselves as socially acceptable, upstanding members of our local culture. We must visualize ourselves as the militant *counterculture* Jesus expects. Allowing Satan's monkey wrench of tradition to jam the gears, assures impotence. If, in the name of freedom, we throw out the rules, anarchy and chaos will shake us apart...bits of us flying everywhere.

What is the answer? Be absolutely under the authority of Jesus as expressed in God's inspired Word, and that authority *only.*[13] Let us be efficient, orderly, and pleasing to God by respecting the rules. At the same time, let soaring winds of creative thinking blowing on wings of responsible Christian freedom lift us to unprecedented altitudes. Let us soar upward, finding new ways to permeate the universe with the essence and influence of Jesus.

The Problem of Professionalism

I mean no offense by pointing out something all serious students of the Bible and church history acknowledge, however grudgingly: the church in its original form had no clergy/laity distinctions. Yes, there were bishops. Their leadership, however, was a matter of the flock's submission to mature judgment[14]. Furthermore, there was always a plurality in every city until much later. Yes, there were deacons and deaconesses, but they were strictly servants of the church (which is, of course, what "deacon" means) and not office holders. They preached the gospel to every nation in those simple, primitive conditions.[15] Christian influence penetrated every human institution.

Students of history are aware of the story of the rise of the bishops, archbishops, metropolitans and eventually the popes. This marked the beginning of a headlong fall into apostasy (a moving away from scriptural authority) transforming what had been the church into something Jesus and the apostles would have difficulty recognizing. Since movements to reform the church have seldom gone to the extent of completely purging the remnants of apostasy, the problem lingers.

Professionalism exists as a residue of apostasy, no matter what name you give it. For example, most churches participate in larger governing organizations (synods, conferences, conventions, councils) with certain standards and theological requirements, *overseen by professionals*. Where do we find such an arrangement in Scripture? Even within local congregations a professional with a title (sometimes with the approval of a board of deacons or elders) "calls the shots." To this day, several denominations retain hierarchies reminiscent of their Roman Catholic origins. Jesus could not have addressed the matter more clearly.

> *Jesus said to them, "The kings of the Gentiles lord it over them; and those who exercise authority over them call themselves Benefactors. But you are not to be like that. Instead, the great*

> *est among you should be like the*
> *youngest, and the one who rules*
> *like the one who serves." (Luke*
> *22:25,26)*

The prices we pay for such departures from the original pattern are major roadblocks to fulfillment of our mission *another monkey wrench!*

In the late 18th Century, some very capable men led early reform movements on what was then the Western Frontier of the United States. Granted, they were of very different character, temperament, personality and background. They agreed, however, on one point: a strong dislike for the idea of paid, professional preachers. Now, I don't consider paid preachers unscriptural. I'm not even saying this because I *am* one! The Word okays men making their living from the gospel.[16] In the same paragraph I want to maintain that *professionalism* has been harmful to the church. We have created an unruly monster in self-promoting persons who climb ecclesiastical ladders, playing the game of musical churches, always striving to rise in their income and ego. Howard Norton concurs,

> Unbridled, personal ambition among those who preach or lead is a constant threat to the church. It has always been and always will be.
>
> For Jesus, there was no excuse for mixing the service of God and personal ambition. Greatness, according to Jesus, was to be found in serving others and not in position, power or title.
>
> Preachers, perhaps more than any other group in the church have trouble remembering and practicing this truth.
>
> Preachers on the lectureship circuit

who work in big, rich, sophisticated churches appear to be especially vulnerable to Satan's seductive power.[17]

Self-promotion should be taboo for Christians. Obviously, there are legitimate reasons for getting one's name before the public. It is very difficult, for example, to do intercongregational work such as specialized seminars, without publicity and promotion. It is difficult to publish and market a book based on the merits of the book alone. The author needs name recognition both through his own reputation for good works. He needs the recommendation of others who may be better known. If one has something to sell, then one must market it.

Self-serving, egotistical self-promotion becomes another matter entirely. I believe most of us can tell the difference. We need to *blow the whistle* on any system requiring us to *blow our horn!* Positions or levels of prestige obliging us to boast and campaign like some politician contradict Jesus' teaching about greatness in the kingdom of heaven.[18]

Most preachers I know abhor politics. They feel burdened enough with motivating and involving their congregations. They don't want power or prestige; they simply want to fulfill the work of an evangelist. And so, it always amazes me that even in the church we see people jockey for positions imagined to be influential, lucrative and powerful.

Many, like most of our all-too-visible political campaigners, seem very busy promoting themselves. Some spend years getting higher degrees. Accumulating publicity, in the process of clambering for appointments to the largest churches and most prestigious pulpits, absorbs them. Consequently, they neglect their legitimate mission. They have more concern for *reputation* than *redemption*...more interest in the way to the top rather than the way of the cross. What a shameful, wasteful, tragedy! Meanwhile, the gospel is withheld from millions.

Jesus built his church with no stairs to the top — only steps leading down to true greatness, a greatness not found in the penthouse of ambition, but in the basement of service. Ultimately, fellow preachers, it will not matter where we have preached. It will only matter whom we have preached![19] It will mean nothing that we have stood in prestigious pulpits. It will only matter that we have gained entrance into human hearts and minds.

Whether we have stood before kings and queens in sumptuous palaces or before primitive tribes in jungle clearings, the same simple, beautiful, powerful message of grace alone will count. Remember Paul? He had it all: breeding, background, education, reputation...he ditched it like sewage because he knew its true worth. He knew the real value lay in knowing his Lord Christ Jesus and preaching his gospel.[20]

Now here is the point: we will never meet the ideal of the priesthood of all believers as long as we continue to see equipping, edifying and evangelizing as the work of *professionals*. Unless we see *each member* as a minister and necessary to the functioning as the body of Christ, spiritual muscles will atrophy. They will become immobile, auditors whose primary contribution consists of increasing attendance figures.

Evangelism especially suffers under such an arrangement. Lost souls cannot wait for the overworked and overloaded professional evangelist to arrive on the scene like some sanctified super-hero to save the day. If we continue to think of spreading the good news about Jesus as something better left to professionals, our neighbors will continue to die unsaved. The monkey wrench of professionalism not only *jams the gears,* but *kills and destroys.*

How do we change? For some religious groups it

requires stripping back the layers of man-made tradition. It will mean chipping away the corrosion of the centuries. Ah! A true reformation at last! For others, less burdened by the sediment of the ages, it will be a matter of honest self-examination. It will mean a re-investigation of Scripture followed by restructuring. Groups consisting of autonomous congregations will have to refuse to play musical pulpits any longer. They must deprive professional climbers of their ladders.

Consider your full-time preacher. Usually underpaid and working alone, requirements on his time exceed reality. Then he's "put out to pasture" with little or no retirement benefits just when his experience, wisdom, and ability are at their peak. No wonder ladders look attractive! Why not make ladders obsolete through honest efforts to take care of our full-time ministers?

We can make giant strides toward solving the problem of professionalism by returning to the simple New Testament teaching of the priesthood and servanthood of all believers. Abandonment of those principles caused the rise of professionalism. Let those who aspire to positions of power and prestige do so without our aid.

May we cast off suits of ambition in favor of the towel of service. Let us follow the one who washed the sweat and dust of Palestine from the feet of his disciples. Disciples who, like us, needed to learn what it meant to acquire a servant's heart and serve...*just serve.*[21]

The Future of the Central Church

Will Mike's church remain Satan's victory and Heaven's casualty? If it remains typical of most inert churches, the answer is *yes*. Someone in Mike's town will begin a dynamic new work. They will draw members from Central and other comatose churches.

I prefer to think, however, the Central church will not be typical. Pulling the monkey wrenches from the machinery, the gears will again turn, meshing together in unity. First, Mike will have to really decide to follow Jesus and him only. That initial decision will fill him with purpose, focus and enthusiasm. As he revives his sleeping brothers and sisters, the Central church may again receive the empowering candlestick of Jesus. It will regain consciousness, rekindle the fire of the Holy Spirit. Then, once more, it will become a beacon whose beams of light penetrate the surrounding darkness.

[1] 2 Corinthians 11:14
[2] 2 Corinthians 2:10,11
[3] Acts 20:28
[4] Galatians 5:13
[5] Romans 6:15
[6] Galatians 3:11
[7] Hebrews 8:13
[8] F. LaGard Smith, *The Cultural Church*, 20th Century Christian, 2809 Granny White Pike, Nashville, TN 37204, 1992, p. 42

114 Monkey Wrenches

[9]Acts 20:7

[10]The position is that *heautois* (Eph. 5:9) and *heautous* (Col. 3:16) mean all the congregation singing at one time. The argument made is that one person or group cannot sing to another listening in silence because it eliminates reciprocal singing. But does it? To replace congregational singing with a soloist or ensemble would clearly be an error. It seems plain enough, however, that if a soloist or ensemble sings a song to the church at one time and the church all sings together at another (as indeed they must according to the passages in Ephesians and Colossians) this is reciprocal. Are we fulfilling the purpose of singing? That is the question. Is the Lord being praised with thankfulness? Are the saints teaching, admonishing, speaking to one another?

[11]Monroe Hawley, *Redigging the Wells,* Quality Publications, Abilene, 1976, pp 168, 169.

[12]Hebrews 13:8

[13]It is necessary to point out here that it is not part of our job to police the brotherhood or other fellowships in order to expose those congregations we believe to be *violating* scriptural authority. We waste tremendous amounts of time and energy being distracted by stuff that, even if it is any of our business, we can do little about.

[14]This is most certainly the way it should be today but seldom is.

[15]Romans 10:18; 16:26 and Colossians 1:6

[16]1 Corinthians 9:1-14

[17]Howard Norton, editorial, THE CHRISTIAN CHRONICLE, February 1995, p. 18

[18]Matthew 18:4; Luke 22:26

[19]I Corinthians 1:23; 2 Corinthians 4:5

[20]Philippians 3:8

[21]John 13:5ff

9

NATURAL EVANGELISM

It Was Work!

At this point, I must ask for your patience because when I speak of evangelism, it is necessary to write about what I have personally experienced. Thus, I'll be making references to events occurring primarily among churches of Christ. If you'll bear with me, you will, no doubt, find many parallels in your own fellowship.

Back in the dim mists of prehistory (the 1950's) when I was a teenager, "Cottage Meetings" (in-home Bible Studies) were all the rage. A very creative man, Jule Miller, came out with his famous filmstrips. Churches bought several sets, the projectors, and screens to show them. Churches held "personal work" classes teaching folks how to use them and the "Tisdel Charts."

Out in the oil field towns of West Texas, although we had eaten our share of cottage cheese, didn't know a "cottage" from a tank farm. However, for about the next ten to fifteen years, "Cottage Meetings," using filmstrips, were reaching the lost and acquainting a lot of oil-patch people with classical religious art. And you know, it worked! Record numbers of conversions took place using this excellent method. Trouble was...it was work!

Too soon, people got tired of carrying all that stuff around. Besides, it was getting harder and harder to "find prospects" to set up studies with. Between you and me, I believe the real problem was the "new" began to wear off. For those willing to make even a small effort, the method remains extremely effective. An updated version on video tape is selling well.

A few years later, we caught the "bus bug", touted as the definitive way of reaching the lost. Didn't Jesus say to go out into the *highways* and byways and compel them to come in?[1] A church simply bought two or more used school buses, cleaned and painted them up, staffed them with a driver, teacher, and song-leader, started running them around the neighborhood. Presto! Rolling Sunday schools! This was something the Baptists and their kin had been doing for a long time because of their emphasis upon building the Bible school. It worked! Our Sunday schools were *huge!* We filled them with red and yellow black and white, just as the song says. Sometimes the kids and their folks came to Christ. Trouble was, it was *work!* A lot of people spent a lot of time without a lot of encouragement and support. Soon, the workers burned out and dropped out. Bus programs passed out of favor. These days, churches with bus programs are rare.

Along with the buses, there were personal evangelism "campaigns." Invented for fearless folks outgoing enough to get with a group, select a community, and knock doors like crazy. The workers usually used filmstrips or some kind of Bible study guide like the Open Bible Study pioneered by Ivan Stewart. These *also worked!* In 1972 our congregation in

Adelaide, Australia, had a campaign led by Stewart and sponsored by a church in Arlington, Texas. It must have been one of the most successful campaigns on record. It pushed our work ahead by years. Trouble was, it was work! Today extremely efficient campaigns continue under several auspices but not nearly at the same level.

One bright, shining star gives a new twist to an old method. Begun by a remarkable man, Jimmy Lovell, it is an incredibly successful correspondence course that has won multiplied thousands of souls in the developing nations, the former Soviet, and Eastern bloc nations. Fittingly named "World Bible School," it consists of hundreds of Christians, including many retired folks, conducting a simple Bible class by correspondence. A teacher may have dozens of students who, through a simple study about Christ and his church, have come to faith. So successful has this method been, workers in the field find it difficult to contact converts. Far from reaching its full potential, this program, now under the direction of Tex Williams, constantly seeks to enlist more teachers for the exploding number of students. Again, it is *work!*

In my own fellowship, programs such as World Radio,We Care, Herald of Truth and other, more regional efforts staffed by hard-working, visionary leaders, reach the masses. People answering Jesus' call to make disciples need to remember we follow him who suffered physically, emotionally and spiritually in his quest for souls.

Recently, hundreds of gospel preachers and teachers are taking advantage of the removal of a rusty iron curtain to bring the gospel of Christ to the lost sheep of the house of Marxism-Leninism. Capitalizing on a widespread desire to learn English, they offer classes using the Bible as a textbook. Thousands have enrolled, learned of God's grace, responded in faith. Congregations by the hundreds have sprung into existence across the former Soviet Union and erstwhile client nations. This thrust with the Spirit's sword into the very heart of atheistic humanism continues with no let-up in sight.

When you look at the domestic scene in the United States, Europe, and Australia, many stars are still visible but much harder to find and light years apart. Many outstanding congregations, busy permeating their world with the saving message of Christ, understand that bringing the good news of Jesus to others too often becomes more a matter of *tongue* than *deed*. Someone put it this way: "When all is said and done, a lot more is said than done." Truer words are seldom spoken! We have turned into a religion that *says* far more than it *does*. We must have less *talk* and more *action*.

It worries us that great evangelistic thrusts are matters of history instead of current events. Dr. Billy Graham appears to be sole survivor of the great campaigns and rallies of the past. In my own fellowship, no one has arisen to replace the great Jimmy Allen, whose stadium-filling crusades resulted in tremendous numbers of responses in the 50s and 60s. Now, only a few outstanding congregations practice outreach on a large scale. While this may seem unfortunate, we must not put the eggs of our understanding of outreach in such little baskets. Australian Alan Bailey has observed,

> ...for many, both inside and outside the church, the image of an outstanding individual persuading masses of people about their need for God is the beginning and ending of their understanding of evangelism.

Studies, said Bailey, have shown the earth's billions will never hear the gospel if we rely on great crusades to do it. Evangelism must be a process of multiplying our efforts. Each Christian must disciple others who disciple others who disciple others or the masses of earth will remain in darkness.[2] We don't need another "personal work class" included in next quarter's curriculum! We need to shut the classroom doors and take it to the streets. Filmstrips? Buses? Campaigns? Correspondence courses? Television? Just do it!

Static-cling Christianity

Presently, across the domestic religious landscape we drift, caught in some kind of "evangelistic doldrums." Many home congregations have turned inward. Content to become "magnet churches" they attract and accumulate those who are already believers as they move into the community or become disenchanted with their former "church home."

Activity produces static electricity. People are attracted by all the sparks. The local church too often sees this "static-cling" phenomenon as success. To be sure, it's very complimentary to any congregation when folks moving to the community choose to be a part. The obvious success of these churches attracts many non believers and unchurched, especially if there is a flat line on their own congregation's enthusiasm and involvement meter. Hopefully, they will become faithful, committed Christians through this association. But, strictly speaking, this is *not outreach.*

We need to apply some simple arithmetic! If someone leaves one church to become a part of another, a congregation somewhere else has lost a worker. In the overall scheme of things, a net-gain of zero for the kingdom. In this ball game, people haven't been *saved,* they've simply been *traded.* The real mark of success comes when we sow the gospel and God blesses our effort with a great harvest of rescued souls.

Currently, among some churches, we see evidence of a resurging tide of interest in reaching others creeping up the domestic shore. Though many have, in fact, recalled their missionaries (in tough economic times, they are always the most expendable) they look at their own communities realizing, all along, the mission field was next door too!

As the pagan understanding of morality in the "developed nations" becomes fuzzier, contrast between the kingdoms of light and darkness becomes sharper. For example, our present generation has turned to the snake oil of materialism as an elixir to soothe their frazzled nerves. Unfortunately, "A man who has set out to serve both God and Mammon soon discovers that there is no God."[3] On the upside, as the contrast increases, so do opportunities. People who have tried everything are beginning to ask that age-old question, "Is this all there is?" The communities of this newly sated society are ripening fields. We must roll in the combines before they become too rotten for harvest.

Outreach Is a Personal Matter

Our mission: go, preach, make disciples, baptize, teach, seek and save...has usually been understood in a *collective* sense; something we do *together.* But, if the corporate body ever does anything, it will be a matter of *individual* commitment to it. So often, we respond to needs by hiring someone to take care of them. There's nothing wrong with that unless it becomes a one-man job.

Every leader has experienced the frustration and irritation of having a brother or sister point out something that "ought to be done," with absolutely no intention of being a part of the doing. It is easier to see the needs than to recognize the necessity of our involvement in meeting them.

The New Testament depicts the fellowship of saints as *individual* disciples militantly penetrating their world with the way, truth and life of their Master. Their hope was evident. They were ready to *explain* it and *live* it.[4] My choice of the word "militantly" is not off-handed. Again, we have a defensive "fortress mentality" when we ought to have an offensive militant one.

In the Holy Spirit's eyes, we are *individual* soldiers, not a platoon. We are to fight primarily with our own personal weapons, not just as a "gun crew." We must stop seeing the sharing of Jesus as primarily a *corporate* matter. Evangelism, even in a packed stadium, eventually becomes a matter of one person communicating with another.

Charles Spurgeon's description of evangelism was "One beggar telling another where to find bread." A friendly and concerned group of Christians will have a positive impact upon someone. Yes, people may be stirred by the singing and moved by the prayers. But, sooner or later, the gospel must enter mind and heart to do the Spirit's convicting and motivating work. Several may share in the work of transmitting that gospel, but touching others with God's grace will always be one-at-a-time.

Each Christian has a realm of influence, a world into which Jesus commanded us to go. Each Christian has a supply of seed (the Word of God), and a field (our world) into which to sow it. Family, friends, neighbors, fellow-workers, associates at school, associates in recreational activities and community service are soil in which to sow seed. Only a hermit has no field. Even then, the only hermit I ever knew still received mail, was required to vote (in Australia), and lived on canned fish and milk delivered by the postman.

If we penetrate and permeate our culture as salt,[5] we will do it as individual crystals. If we are the light that penetrates the darkness,[6] we will do it as individual rays. If we are the leaven of the kingdom that infuses itself into society,[7] we will do it as individual lumps. Fading into obscurity as we imitate and emulate the world around us has never been the mode of operation for committed Christians.

From the very beginning, Christians have aggressively taken their place in contemporary culture. Tertullian, a Christian author writing about 155 to 222 years after the birth of Christ, says it best:

> We are a new group but have already penetrated all areas of imperial life — cities, islands, villages, towns, marketplaces, even the camp, tribes, palace, senate, law-court. There is nothing left for you but your temples.[8]

Those early Christians did this, of course, *individually*, not *collectively*. Groups of people sitting in church buildings do not make progress like this. Only when I understand, as an individual, I *personally* must go into the world, will the feats of our ancient brethren be equaled or excelled.

Actually, I have never known a soul-winner who worked primarily with a group. They are ordinary folks...some physically challenged in one way or another. One of the most effective evangelists I have ever known was a janitor on the campus at Texas Women's University. It seemed there was always some young lady in the dormitory where he worked being immersed into Christ. He didn't wait for a "personal work" program; he *was* the program! He was not taking refuge in a fortress. He was out engaging the enemy taking every thought captive to the obedience of Christ.[9] To top it all off...he had a most profound stutter!

I know another man who teaches Christians how to be soul-winners. Both optically and auricularly dyslexic, he sees and hears words backwards. Don Calhoun doesn't let that stop him. One can almost sense that he, like the apostle Paul before him, takes pleasure in overcoming these challenges for the sake of souls. Now, what is *our* excuse?

How Will They Hear?

The necessity of contact with the non-Christian goes without saying. Giving a wide berth to the world is an example of not thinking like Jesus. You would think, in the process of seeking the lost, it would dawn on us the "lost" are as much the pimps and their prostitutes[10] as they are law-abiding, squeaky-clean, upright but unchurched folks in our neighborhood. Bailey nails it again, writing:

> Here we touch the raw nerve of our failure in evangelism today. Contact with those around us in our world is so minimal. When someone is added to our church by conversion, he very soon loses all his old acquaintances and becomes one of us — people who are comfortable with those of like mind and highly uncomfortable about getting too close to the non-Christian.[11]

Who are the people the gospel can call? They are people just like you and me who are *open* to the gospel. Alcoholics, workaholics, substance abusers, people abusers thieves, con-artists, the greedy, the immoral, homosexuals, adulterers, the poor, the rich, the disenfranchised, the unskilled, the poorly educated, and the outcasts. Paul reminds the arrogant Corinthian church:

> *Brothers, think of what you were when you were called. Not many of you were wise by human standards; not many were of noble birth. But God chose the foolish things of the world to shame the strong. He chose the lowly things of this world and the despised things--and the things that are not -- to nullify the things that are, so that no one may boast before him.[12]*

Who will talk to these people? Who will dare to enter their turf? Who will eat with them? Who will pay the price of becoming like them in order to win some to Christ?[13] Some of the most challenging and adventure-filled mission fields are right under our noses. Perhaps we fail to see them because we point our noses in a direction blinding us to opportunity. But *there they are!* No, don't turn away! Look upon the ghettos of poverty and crime hidden in the folds of our deceptively gleaming cities. Look upon them with the eyes of Jesus, and *weep!*

Mission Work

We usually reserve the term "mission work," for any work far away where we support the preacher. Even then, we tend to be assembly oriented. For example, when involved in overseas evangelism, one of my supporting congregations asked for monthly reports including attendance and contribution figures compared with that same month in the previous year. They never visited the field, never questioned the effectiveness of the methods I used, or made suggestions. They wanted results. The implication was clear: if there were not enough, support would be cut-off without analysis or investigation.

I recently read another church's guidelines for their mission work which expressed disappointment in two of their undertakings. They recently dropped one because, "The people of that country are not receptive." But since when is that any of *our* business? Never did Jesus imply we should "Go into all the world and preach the gospel to the *receptive.*"

Using that criterion, by the way, would eliminate many works in our own communities. Shall I recount the stories of Noah, Ezekial, Jerimiah, and others sent to preach to people known beforehand to be unresponsive? "Getting results" is

God's business. He sends us to "preach the gospel" because that's our business.

Are we failures if we don't get "results?" If we mean by "results," *baptisms*, then we join a long list of "failures" including Jesus, John the Baptist, the apostle Paul, and most local churches. Paul had a hard time keeping track of who he baptized (1 Corinthians 1:13-17). He emphasized *advancing the gospel* by whatever means possible.

If you've communicated even a tiny portion of the gospel to someone outside the kingdom, *you are an unqualified success!* The Holy Spirit quite capably takes the words we speak and fills them with His power. Paul knew the power was not within him. He referred to himself and Apollos as *opportunity givers* laboring under the full understanding that it is God who causes the growth.[14] I am not aware of *any* place where the gospel, communicated to the people in a *credible, valid* way, has not produced conversions.

Our concern *should* be (both in foreign and domestic endeavors): is the gospel effectively getting across to the people? God's word will not return to him void. People *will* be saved. Let's do *our* job and let God do *his*.

Now *That's* Evangelism!

Susie & Darryl

As Elaine arrived to pick up her son, Susie noticed the tears in her eyes. Over the months of running her in-home child care service, she grew fond of the attractive young mother. She asked Elaine if she wanted to talk about it, and since this was in Australia, they sat down for a "cuppa." Elaine poured out her heart while Sue poured out the tea. She told Susie she was leaving her husband over a multitude of problems.

The dammed-up fear, resentment and pain were more than she could hide. Furthermore, he recently pulled a gun and implied he would harm himself and/or her if sufficiently provoked. Because Elaine was afraid, Susie and her husband Darryl, opened their home to her. She gratefully accepted their refuge.

During her stay, she observed their Christian home in action. She was impressed enough to attend worship assembly the following Sunday. In the meantime, Darryl became acquainted with Elaine's husband. Over the space of a few days, was able to share the gospel with him. Later, Darryl immersed him in one of the member's swimming pools. Now *that's* evangelism...pure, unadorned, life-and-need related, Christ-centered evangelism.

Will Elaine's marriage survive? Will her husband remain faithful to the Lord? No one knows but the Father. We *do know* a couple of precious souls heard the gospel. Circumstances raised a window of opportunity. For one brief, shining moment, they were open to the gospel Darryl and Susie eagerly share with anyone who will listen.

Gary

It was, as we say in Texas, stinkin' hot. The young family stranded in the run-down car on the shoulder of a busy freeway felt every sizzling degree. The husband tried to phone for help. Everyone he knew was unavailable for several hours. Meanwhile, the impartial sun boiled down on the hungry baby, the exhausted wife, and the despairing young husband.

That's when a disciple of Christ named Gary Dacke just happened to be passing. He pulled over and took the risk of involving himself in their misery. Gary, an airline mechanic, soon discovered the fuel pump had squirted its last and needed replacing. He took the mother and baby to their home.

Then, he and the husband went to the nearest automotive parts store.

The part cost more money than the young man had. Gary gladly purchased the part, returned to the car, replaced the pump and got the grateful young father back on the road. In response to the man's questions, Gary was able to explain he was a follower of Christ and just trying to "go about doing good," as did his Master.[15]

The young man seemed impressed with this, and Gary did his best to maintain contact. But to this day, as far as Gary knows, his act of kindness has not resulted in any further spiritual progress. Gary rests in the knowledge that seed was sown. Now *that's* evangelism! Was Gary successful? You betcha!

Roy and Alma

Roy Hillman is a man with many burdens. One of those burdens is the spread of the gospel in his adopted country of Australia. In spite of mediocre health, he and his wife, Alma (though well past the age of retirement), are always trying to help several family members also in poor physical health. Consequently, they spend a great deal of their time recovering from exhaustion. They live in the old South Australian mining town of Kapunda, and we correspond four or five times a year. I got a letter from him one day full of the usual news. At the end, he excitedly wrote:

> Oh yes! Oh yes! This is what I really wanted to let you know two weeks ago. There was a big rally of old cars and buses and trucks in Adelaide — two forty-year-old buses came over from Sydney. I was asked if I would like to travel all around Adelaide and on to St. Kilda. This I did, and I enjoyed it. I

> also met a man who was searching for the truth (he too was interested in old vehicles). But instead of talking Buses and Trains, etc., I talked to him about (Christ and his church). We talked and talked for three hours on that old Sydney bus. So we can find people almost anywhere. I was glad I was there and so was he. He and I...talked later on the phone. He was well accepted by all at Salisbury (church) last Sunday.

Roy and Alma have a heart for God! They host a tiny church in their Kapunda home and love their brothers and sisters in Christ. They are, by definition, senior citizens. But most of all, they are citizens of the kingdom. As natural as breathing, Roy talks about Jesus and his church. Now *that's* evangelism!

Sharing Christ, to really be effective on a long-term basis, must be *natural*. It can only become natural to us when it becomes *important* enough we begin to *think like Jesus*. To one for whom reaching out has become natural, *everything becomes a tool*...the car, the home, money, time and energy. Natural evangelists use these tools without hesitation when souls are at stake because they are *serious!*

George Barna, in his study of successful churches, tells us they are full of people who are *serious* about reaching others.

> These were people who were passionate about outreach. They were more than simply happy to be doing the Lord's work; they were inspired. Their perspective was that nothing could be more important than enabling others to understand Scripture, to make a commitment to Jesus Christ and to grow in their faith.

> They saw every event in their lives as
> having a hand in better enabling them to
> reach others for Christ. They looked
> upon life as an opportunity to serve
> God.[16]

What makes these people different? Why are some passionate
for souls and others content to "do church?" Barna says,
"...they recognized that being a part of a body of believers that
is on fire to transform the world is a blessing that could not be
matched."[17]

Our main problem is not "How?" but "Why?" We act
unconvinced that, outside of Christ, *people are lost*.[18] Have
we forgotten the Smith family next door needs Jesus as much
as we do? We conveniently "forget" that, outside of Christ, the
Smith family faces the horrors of eternal damnation. But worst
of all, perhaps we have not yet fallen in love with Jesus, the
one who saved us from the same fate.

Back in 1981, an Irish prisoner by the name of Bobby
Sands starved himself to death. He and several other members
of the Irish Republican Army had gone on a hunger strike to
publicize their cause and their commitment to it. Was their
cause a just one? Did Bobby Sands die in vain? While you
ponder those questions, notice the level of commitment he and
the other hunger-strikers exhibited.

It's not easy to starve to death. Anyone who has fasted
for a period of time will tell you it can be painful. If you starve
yourself long enough, certain organs begin to break down
irreparably. Mr. Sands endured the pain of starving for over
two months! Why? Obviously, he *believed* in what he was
starving for. Before his imprisonment, he risked his life *fighting* for it. He was willing to live and die for his cause, something rare in a time of commitments with the consistency of
warm gelatin.

The cause of Christ has its heroes: dedicated, committed men and women willing to risk health, life and earthly happiness for the Master. Sadly, however, even Christian heroism is the *exception* rather than the *rule.* Why is this?

Oh, we *agree* Jesus is the Son of God who died to free us from sin...but do we really believe the vast majority of the billions of inhabitants of the world are lost unless they obey the good news? Do we really believe *only Jesus* can bring peace to this war-torn planet? Do we believe *only Jesus* can give people an abundant life filled with purpose? If we *really believe* these things, we are acting strangely.

How can members of a fellowship claiming to be the "pillar and support of the truth" remain content with pew warming and nice little fattening socials? How can we listen to teachers and preachers urging commitment and action, then dismiss them as over-zealous fanatics or mere professionals doing what they're *paid* to do? We don't need *suicide,* we need *sacrifice*—living sacrifices of transformed people zealous to prove what the will of God is, that which is good and acceptable and perfect.[19] We need to get as serious about Jesus and his kingdom as Bobby Sands was about Irish Republicanism. He was *dead serious.*

My friend, if you are not filled with a serious sense of urgency for the lost surrounding you, *something is wrong.* Get into the Word. Let the Holy Spirit diagnose the problem and let the Great Physician heal you! The urgent revolution must begin in your heart.

[1]Luke 14:23
[2]Alan Bailey, *Good News Down Under,* Anzea Publishers, 3-5Richmond Road, Homebush West, NSW 2140, Australia, 1992, p. 11

3Logan Pearsall Smith as quoted in *Comatose Christianity,* by Ron Carlson, Christian Communications, Nashville, 1989, p. 90

[4]1 Peter 3:15

[5]Matthew 5:13

[6]Matthew 5:14

[7]Matthew 13:33

[8]Tertullian, *Apology,* v:6; xxxvii:4,5; xlii:2,3 as quoted by Everett Ferguson, *Early Christians Speak,* pp. 219,220, Sweet Publishing Company, Austin, Texas, 1971.

[9]Colossians 2:8 and 2 Corinthians 10:4,5

[10]Matthew 21:31

[11]Alan Bailey, Op. Cit., p. 61

[12]I Corinthians 1:26-29 NIV

[13] 1 Corinthians 9:19-21?

[14] 1 Corinthians 3:5

[15]Acts 10:38

[16]George Barna, *User Friendly Churches,* Regal Books, Division of GL Publications, Ventura, California, 1991, p. 36.

[17]Ibid., p. 36

[18]Ephesians 2:1-5 and many others.

[19]Romans 12:1,2

10

THE DREAMING

Corroboree

The sun dropped below the horizon leaving only a deep red glow to silhouette the low hills. In a depression between some dunes of blood-red sand, other silhouettes moved around a large, crackling fire. The drone of didgeridoos[1] and the clack of boomerangs backed-up several men whose eerie singing accompanied the dancers. Their ochre-painted bodies writhed as their stomping corroboree dance stirred little puffs of sand around their feet.

A short distance away from this stone age scene, Europeans and Asians fill 20th Century cities. In the dances and traditions of the Australian Aborigine, they remember the time of creation over and over. They refer to this as "the dreaming," or the "dreamtime" when super humans and animals created the strange, beautiful and unique landscape of Australia.

No doubt the term "dreaming" comes from the dreams and visions of these first inhabitants of Australia as they sought explanations for the features of their new homeland. We always, after all, associate dreams with new beginnings...with times of creation. The church in the late twentieth century must begin our dreamtime. We must essentially look to our first beginnings if we are going to enter "the dreaming" of new beginnings.

The Possibilities

I may be overly fond of dreaming. In elementary school, a regular complaint inscribed on my report card was, "Day-dreams too much." Dreaming is possible alone and almost anywhere. Furthermore, provided it is not on the boss's time, it is absolutely free. I speak of visions of *great actions and accomplishments*...not the lazy day-dreaming people engage in during sermons. Martin Luther King Jr. was a dreamer with a vision of Americans of all races standing proud, free and prosperous. He didn't just *dream* about it; he *worked* for it. He wrote, spoke, marched, demonstrated, persuaded, and traveled constantly for it. At the last, he took a bullet for it. I am confident, were he still alive today; he would keep on going. I believe with all my heart God wants men and women to have *visions* today; visions of greatness in his glorification!

I have a dream I want to share with you, a *really big* dream of a God-glorifying, Christ-exalting, soul-saving, disciple-making, *victorious* church! An impossible dream? I don't think so. Now, lie back on your bed or sit in your recliner or stretch out on the sofa. Dream a dream with me. After all, this is *scriptural!*[2]

A Powerful Church

First, let's think about the power of Yahweh channeled through the Word in the creation of the universe. Consider the vastness of its space. Consider the awesome power of billions of nuclear fires concentrated in galaxies, clusters and constellations. Consider the term "light-year." Think about how long it takes the light of the nearest star to twinkle in our sky. Think about the One who, by his incomprehensible power binds it all altogether.

Now think about the earthly expressions of His power: our fearful and wonderful construction,[3] the flood, the deliverance of Israel from Egypt, the pillars of cloud and fire, the manna, the giving of the Law, the mighty words and works of the prophets. Finally, consider the birth of a Messiah, his life, teachings, and resurrection from the dead. Consider the *power* behind all these wonders. Now, ponder the most mind-expanding thought of all: *we have access to this power!*[4]

Next, let's consider our mission as fellow workers with God. Think of the magnitude of the task of preaching the gospel to all creation.[5] Think of the struggle required to leaven and enlighten our world with the teachings and principles of the Master. Now, before we throw up our hands in despair, let's remember the achievements of the past. Because of Paul's letter to the Colossians, we know the entire known world heard the gospel once before.[6] Yes, it was a much smaller world, but the work-force was much smaller too.

How *remarkable* a small group of largely uneducated men, gathered, trained, and taught by an itinerant Jewish preacher, successfully penetrated and permeated the cultures and civilizations of that time! They turned the world upside down![7]

Let your mind run free to dream *beyond* past accomplishments! Dream of the gospel preached to *billions.* Visualize all levels and strata of society in all cultures and civilizations penetrated by the enlightened morals and ethics of Jesus Christ. Imagine good works that comfort, feed, and clothe the poverty and famine stricken all over the world.

Picture a world so saturated with the message of the Prince of Peace that war is intolerable. Conceive of a world where the mere pressure of Christian morals forces sexual exploitation and perversion to cower in the darkest corners and closets. In your reverie, can you depict a business climate permeated by Christian ethics in which trust and honor are the rule? How about a world of strong, functional families, with rare divorce? Can you conceive of a world celebrating and enjoying racial and ethnic characteristics instead of making them the focus of bigotry and hatred?

Okay, you can wake up now...*but don't forget the dream!* Let me tell you a little secret: we have not dreamed a single impossible dream. Call me an idealist (you won't be the first). Call me crazy. Call me irresponsible. But before you do, *think about the power.*

How many times have you heard it (or a variation of it): "What the mind can conceive and the heart can believe, the will can achieve." When we talk of prayer and available power, we're talking *way beyond* conceive, believe, and achieve.[8] We're looking at *colossal* power unlimited by our puny mental capacity to grasp. In this revolution, we must believe in *power.* We must give credence to the power of our righteous cause. We need confidence in our spiritual weapons for the right hand and the left.[9] We need conviction of a power equipping us with every need for sowing the seed.[10] We must have intense confidence in a power able to take the church to heights never before attained!

Beyond our tendency toward a lack of faith and action, I can't think of any reason why we cannot exceed, in every way, the achievements of the past. Every promise of provision and power endures as valid as ever. What can God do with people who surrender to him, absolutely convinced all necessary resources, strength and power are available to fulfill his

task? There are no English words up to the task of describing
the dynamic...almost explosive...result! It is time the people of
God laid claim to the stockpiles of heaven in the warehouses
of God.

We seem to have made peace with the totally counterproductive notion of *impossibility*. Instead of creatively coming to grips with the task at hand, we stick it on the back burn-
er of our mind. That way, we don't have to think about it until
some silly, idealistic visionary forces us to. Many refer to the
task of evangelizing the billions of our world as "impossible."
I would not want to respond to Jesus with such a faithless
word. The thought of telling the returning Jesus his charge was
unrealistic and unattainable fills me with fear and trembling.

We think of the church that reached its world with the
gospel in legendary, almost reverential terms. We have decided, without basis, we can never *equal*, much less *exceed*, the
exploits of those pioneers of the faith. The very idea almost
constitutes treason and sacrilege! Have we resigned ourselves
to the status of the mediocre ?

One of George Barna's discoveries about successful
churches is the leaders were not afraid to dream or believe in
their dreams.

> Their ability to instill uplifting attitudes in the con-
> gregation grew out of their own belief in God's
> blessing. Their desire to serve Him whole-hearted-
> ly was contagious. How liberating it is, people
> learned, to have such dreams and such faith that
> obstacles simply become creative challenges! How
> refreshing it is to shed one's anxieties and replace
> them with visions of impact![11]

Perhaps a better title for this chapter would have been
"Is Anything Impossible?" When you respond to this question, be careful because Jesus has already answered it. When

the disciples expressed concern about salvation, Jesus replied, "With men this is impossible, but with God all things are possible."[12] A man with an epileptic son pled with Jesus, "But if you can do anything, take pity on us and help us!" And Jesus said to him, "If you can! All things are possible to him who believes."[13] When praying in the garden before his betrayal, Jesus was saying, "Father...everything is possible for you."[14]

The scriptural basis for believing all things are possible is vast. Really, it constitutes a separate study in itself. Let's look at a few passages dreams are made of. They remove any doubt about the possibilities.

> *And this is the confidence which we have before Him, that, if we ask anything according to His will, He hears us. And if we know that He hears us in whatever we ask, we know that we have the requests which we have asked from him.[15]*

> *I can do everything through him who gives me strength.[16]*

> *With this in mind, we constantly pray for you, that our God may count you worthy of his calling, and that by his power he may fulfill every good purpose of yours and every act prompted by your faith. We pray this so that the name of our Lord Jesus may be glorified in you, and you in him, according to the grace of our God and the Lord Jesus Christ.[17]*

> *And my God shall supply all your needs according to His riches in glory in Christ Jesus.[18]*

> *And God is able to make all grace about to you, that always having all sufficiency in everything, you may have an abundance for every good deed; Now he who supplies seed to the sower and bread for food,*

> *will supply and multiply your seed for sowing and increase the harvest of your righteousness.*[19]

> *...for everyone born of God overcomes the world. This is the victory that has overcome the world, even our faith. Who is it that overcomes the world? Only he who believes that Jesus is the Son of God*[20]

> *Now to Him who is able to do exceeding abundantly beyond all that we ask or think, according to the power that works within us...*[21]

Christians or churches denying God's power cannot glorify him! So many are "holding a form of godliness but denying the power of it."[22] Unhappily, many are cold, but a few are *frozen!*[23] Entire congregations exist full of people who go through the motions of being godly. They have no strategy, no plans. They have no goals; and they reach them every day! What a sad commentary on our comfortable, convenient and powerless charade of Christianity! Let the revolution begin! *Dream! Work* for the dream! I dare you!

A Wide-awake Church

Years ago, I saw the motion picture, *Tora! Tora! Tora!* It told the story of the Japanese attack on Pearl Harbor in a very accurate way. The movie strikingly portrayed the totally unprepared condition of the United States. The Japanese advances in the Pacific seemed very far away from home. Everyone was taking it easy on that fateful Sunday morning. The Japanese admiral, educated in the States, knew the dangerously relaxed American defenses would be even *more* relaxed on the "day of rest." The well-planned attack came as a total surprise. After the Japanese planes were safe back on their carrier, there was great rejoicing by everyone except the brilliant admiral. Soberly he said, "I fear we have awakened a sleeping giant and filled him with a terrible resolve." History bears witness to the accuracy of his words.

What an extremely painful and costly way to wake up! It would have saved many lives, and averted much suffering had that "giant" been gently shaken out of dreamland instead of being rudely bashed out of it! Prior to the "Day of Infamy," intelligence had been trying to warn Roosevelt and others of Japanese intentions. Someone either overlooked or mislaid the reports. A crucial cable marked *URGENT* was ignored; filed away for reading on Monday. The fleet drew nearer to the islands. The planes took off. A tragedy of errors, slothfulness and apathy assured Japanese success. Unmanned radar posts and key people asleep on the job made the travesty complete.

Many centuries before Pearl Harbor, in a sleepy, prosperous, and apathetic Samaria, an intelligence agent made one last frenzied attempt to warn the people: "THE ASSYRIANS ARE COMING!" "WAKE UP!" "REPENT!" But the Assyrian advances seemed far away...unimportant. The frustrated prophet, ignored by the sluggish citizens, watched the dust cloud raised by the advancing thousands of the cruel Assyrian army drawing nearer...ever nearer.

The overthrow of Samaria was not because of weakness or ignorance. They had all the power of the universe at their disposal. God consistently warned them through the prophets their lifestyle would not go unheeded and unpunished. With apathetic disregard, they plugged their ears. They hardened their hearts while the tide of disaster crept up on them. It is always thus.

Today, Satan and his army are making covert and crafty advances: first here, then there; slowly...slowly, softly...softly, so as not to alert the sleepy, self-satisfied, and distracted army of God. First he takes a family...then a community...a government...a school...the media...finally the church. Disregarding the reports and warnings of preacher and teacher they cry, "What a doom-merchant!" They plead, "Don't make me feel uncomfortable!"

The conflict seems far away. It appears un-threatening to comfortable sleepers in the pews. Token outreach programs and passionless pulpits pose no threat to the advancing forces of darkness. All the while, inexorably, the day approaches when we will awaken, finding ourselves surrounded by the enemy. Victory will then be painful and hard-won. Say! I have a good idea! Let's wake up *now*. You say you're *tired?* Okay, but remember, Satan never sleeps!

How many battles are lost because an army dismisses its enemy? How many tragedies are averted when soldiers are simply aware of *who* the enemy is and *how* he fights?

Note, for example, the battle of Agincourt. When Henry V declared war on the French in 1415, he sailed to France with an army of 12,000 men. Because of a long siege at Harfleur and terrible weather, his army began to sicken and dwindle in numbers. The French, sure of a decisive victory, blocked his army near the castle of Agincourt with well-armored cavalry. They were apparently ignorant of a very important fact: the remaining 9000 English forces included 8000 long-bowmen.

Terrible storms of yard-long arrows from English long-bows met the charging French. The slaughter was terrible. The French regrouped and charged again. Winston Churchill writes, "But once again the long-bow destroyed all before it...he (Henry V) had decisively broken in open battle at odds of more than three to one the armed chivalry of France."[24]

France had apparently learned nothing from a hundred years of losses to smaller forces. They had every opportunity to know their enemy. Instead, they chose to remain ignorant. When we are unable to learn from history, unwilling to learn about our enemy from valid sources; we are ripe for defeat. Paul counsels the Corinthians to be obedient in all things, "in order that no advantage be taken of us by Satan; for we are not ignorant of his schemes."[25]

The best soldier knows the enemy. God has provided information for the Christian soldier. Peter warns us to "Be on the alert. Your adversary, the devil, prowls about like a roaring lion, seeking someone to devour."[26] Paul exhorts, "Put on the full armor of God, that you may be able to stand firm against the schemes of the devil."[27] The alarm is going off! The church of today, fortified inside her buildings, must awaken! We must *go out* to do informed and intelligent battle with the world forces of this darkness.

A Church that Functions like a Body

> For just as we have many members in one body and all the members do not have the same function, so we, who are many, are one body in Christ and individually members of one another. And since we have gifts that differ according to the grace given us, let each exercise them accordingly.[28]

I dream of a *connected* church where every member understands we are a part of one another. Members who become fully aware that failing to function cripples the body, will learn to value each other. All are aware of the gifts God has given into their stewardship. Teachers are teaching, servers are serving, givers are giving, exhorters are exhorting, leaders are leading, and mercy-givers are going about their work with cheerfulness.[29] They eagerly contribute to the growth and welfare of the body by supplying what God has gifted them to provide...

> *...from whom the whole body, being fitted and held together by that which every joint supplies, according to the proper working of each individual part, causes the growth of the body for the building up of itself in love.*[30]

In my dream, elders actually *shepherd* the flock of God. They are *among* the flock, seeing to the needs of the sheep. Instead of sitting in isolation as a board of directors, they get with the sheep. They lead the way in doing good works. They understand true leadership is a matter of *action*, not *position*.

In my flight of fancy, the deacons actually carry out their functions of service by seeing to the physical administration and welfare of the flock. They make decisions about carpet, paint and pews. They organize, deputize and delegate. They connect with leading people of the congregation to see that all the details necessary to everyday functioning of the body run smoothly.

Wow! Don't wake me up! Look! Can you see it? A body concerned with the spiritual and physical welfare of one another! Brothers and sisters in a kaleidoscope of colors, races, socioeconomic status, and educational levels work and worship together! People, beholding the mutual, reciprocal and sincere love of the disciples of Christ are becoming Christians every day.[31] Is it possible? Can it be? Yes! I absolutely believe we can witness the power of God working through his children as never before. Let us keep dreaming and working for the dream!

A Joy-Filled Church

How can it be that people saved from the guilt and punishment of sin...people with hope...with purpose...can be such sour-pusses? It seems so natural for Christians to come together smiling, laughing and enjoying one another's company. Joy results from sharing faith, hope and love. One of the most visible demonstrations of an inward revolution is an outward expression of joy. Christians should be the most joy-filled people on earth! We are saved! We are adopted by the Father! We have eternal life! We have a family who cares about us! We worship and serve One who undeniably manifests his love toward us!

> *Therefore having been justified by faith, we have peace with God through our Lord Jesus Christ, through whom also we have obtained our introduction by faith into this grace in which we stand; and we exult in hope of the glory of God.*[32]

Many religious groups bill themselves as "Spirit-filled Churches." However, if I read my Bible right, one cannot be a child of God without being filled with the Spirit.[33] Churches are, by divine design and definition, vibrant collections of Spirit-filled people. When Paul found unfilled disciples at Ephesus, he immediately suspected their baptism, and he was right. Their baptism "in the name of the Lord Jesus"[34] corrected the problem.

Since all in covenant relationship with God are indwelt by the Spirit, *joy naturally characterizes their churches.* It was Billy Sunday who pointed out, "If you have no joy in religion, there's a leak in your Christianity somewhere." *Joy* and the *Holy Spirit* are inseparable! Joy is a natural by-product of the Holy Spirit's indwelling, even in times of adversity.[35]

> *And the disciples were continually filled with joy and with the Holy Spirit.*[36]

But the fruit of the Spirit is...joy...[37]

...for the kingdom of God is not eating and drinking, but righteousness and peace and joy in the Holy Spirit.[38]

So I dream of a church that *expresses joy.* Jesus said, *"No one takes your joy away from you."*[39] At times it looks as though someone has done exactly that.

From my study of the early church, I get the distinct impression the times of Christian assembly were informal. The stiffness and "high church" protocol we currently employ is an unfortunate legacy of apostasy. People once were free to express their joy with an occasional "hallelujah!" They sang to *one another.* They smiled at *one another.* Perhaps they sang, *"But let the righteous be glad; let them exult before God; Yes, let them rejoice with gladness."*[40] See that word *exult?* We can't exult with our nose in a song book, singing to the back of someone else's head! Rejoicing and exulting require our *whole being!* Spirit-occupied hearts find expression in joy-filled eyes, loving smiles, and praising lips.

It is hard to exult and rejoice with gladness in most churches. The reluctance of others around us to do the same is intimidating. Who wants to audibly say "Praise the Lord!" among people who look at you as though you stood up and did a belly dance? The call for *"decency and order"*[41] doesn't *suppress* expression, it *expedites* it. Listen to what Paul is saying! Don't let your need to be exuberant outweigh edification.

Obviously, expressions of joy didn't end with the assembly. The disciples carried home glowing embers of joy kindled in the assembly. They took them to work and school. Their pagan neighbors, still struggling in cold darkness and futility, saw the warm glow and desired it. Trapped in hopeless misery, they observed the pervasive joy of Christians. Joy is a tremendously effective evangelistic tool. A joy-filled church is a growing church. People naturally gravitate toward joy. I dream of such a church.

An Influential Church

Our invisible brand of Christianity cannot influence our communities. Where the church is numerically strong, crime rates are obviously just as high as areas where disciples are rare. We have just as many scandals. We suffer from the same lack of moral behavior and ethical conduct. Does that bother you? Me too! What a pitiful spectacle of failure!

Every community should know the church of Jesus for high morals, ethics, faith, and love. So I dream of churches filled with Christians who understand what it means to be beacons of righteousness in the darkness of corruption.

If we were exercising our faith as God has provided and empowered us, we would exert powerfully positive influences on the morals of our communities. Paul told the Ephesian disciples, *"And do not participate in the unfruitful deeds of darkness, but instead even expose them."*[42] Okay, so faithful Christians obey the first part of this injunction. Are we exposing evil deeds? Have we made a truce with the muck-dealers? "You stay away from us, and we'll pretend you don't exist." Do we have the guts to "expose them?"

Churches "strong in the Lord and in the strength of His might,"[43] are churches full of people like Gideon's 300 courageous and faithful warriors. I'll say it right out loud: I'd rather have 300 with faith, courage and vision than 10,000 pew-warmers! The writer of Hebrews borrows the words of Habakkuk to teach courage:

But my righteous one shall live by faith;

*and if he shrinks back, my soul has no
pleasure in him. But we are not of those
who shrink back to destruction, but of
those who have faith in the preserving of
the soul.*[44]

Cowardly believers, afraid to do what God has not only
commanded but given *power and provision* to do, make a terrible admission of faithlessness. Spiritually, we are digging
our own graves in Satan's cemetery. He is ecstatic as he sees
us cowering in our comfort zones pretending all is right with
the world. Our ability to rationalize away all responsibility to
exercise our influence upon the world, tickles him pink.

How can a church become *evangelistic* without becoming *influential?* I dream of fellowships whose baptistry waters
have whitecaps because daily conversions are the rule.
Warning! Hard work precedes this dream! Our community
must know we are *extant* instead of *extinct*. People cannot call
on the name of Jesus unless they believe in him. They are not
going to believe in him without hearing about him. They will
never hear without a messenger![45] *Someone must tell them!* I
don't really want to *talk* about the "Great Commission" any
more. I just want to *fulfill it!*

I dream of churches like these. Dreams, however, as
wonderful as they may be, are not reality. Can they come true?
Is it possible? I believe with all my heart they *can*. However,
I will give up my dream if you can do two simple things. First,
prove to me God does not want the church of our dreams.
Second, show me how I have misunderstood the promises and
provisions to fulfill those dreams. In the meantime...I will continue to dream. Will you dream with me? Good! Let's not
allow the dream to fade away! When we are ready to dream
and then work, when we willing teach, preach, travel and persuade, when we are ready to die for the dream, we'll see our

dream come true.

The outback moon rises over the aboriginal campsite. The dust of corroboree has settled. The glow of a small fire sends long spokes of man-shaped shadows radiating around the sandy depression. They remembered Dreamtime. They honored the time of creation in song and dance. Now, with religious fervor spent in ancient acts of worship, dreamtime fades into desert darkness.

---

[1]Long hollowed-out tree limb, played like a bugle in that different tones are made by compression of the lips. Makes low, growling sounds.
   [2]Psalm 4:4
   [3]Psalm 139:14
   4Ephesians 1:19,20
   [5]Mark 16:15
   [6]Colossians 1:5, 6, 23
   [7]Acts 17:6

[8]Ephesians 3:20

[9]2 Corinthians 6:7

[10]2 Corinthians 9:8-11

[11]George Barna, *User Friendly Churches,* Regal Books, Division of GL Publications, Ventura, California, 1991, p.36.

[12]Matthew 19:26; Mark 10:27; Luke 18:27

[13]Mark 9:22,23 (NASB)

[14]Mark 14:36

[15] 1 John 5:14,15 (NASB)

[16]Philippians 4:13

[17]2 Thessalonians 1:11,12

[18]Philippians 4:19 (NASB)

[19]2 Corinthians 9:8,10 (NASB)

[20]1 John 5:4,5

[21]Ephesians 3:20 (NASB)

[22]2 Timothy 3:5

[23]Someone sadly but humorously referred to the church of today as "God's frozen people."

[24]Winston S. Churchill, *A History of the English Speaking Peoples:The Birth of Britain,* Dodd, Mead & Company, New York, 1956, p. 405.

[25]2 Corinthians 2:11 (NASB)

[26]1 Peter 5:8 (NASB)

[27]Ephesians 6:11 (NASB)

[28]Romans 12:4-6 (NASB)

[29]Romans 12:6-8

[30]Ephesians 4:16 (NASB)

[31]I John 3:18; John 13:35

[32]Romans 5:1,2 (NASB)

[33]Acts 2:38; Romans 8:9-17; Galatians 4:6, et al.

[34]Acts 19:1-6

[35]1 Thessalonians 1:6,7; 1 Peter 1:6-8

[36]Acts 15:32 (NASB)

[37]Galatians 5:22 (NASB)

[38]Romans 14:17 (NASB)

[39]John 16:22 (NASB)

[40]Psalm 68:3 (NASB)

[41] 1 Corinthians 14:40
[42] Ephesians 5:11 (NASB)
[43] Ephesians 6:10 (NASB)
[44] Hebre ws 10:38,39 (NASB)
[45] Romans 10:13-15

11

Let's Get Practical

F ire! The oil in the frying pan was in flames! The panic stricken young bride, not knowing exactly what to do, grabbed the handle and, holding it at arms length, set it down on the floor! There, before dying down, it promptly burnt a hole in the expensive linoleum. The problem, a grease fire, turned into a bigger problem: a charred ring in the floor covering. Because the next mistake could have been even worse, this woman now keeps a fire extinguisher in her kitchen. She is wise enough to deal with the problem by proper preparation.

To expose problems, discuss them, and *discard* them makes them grow bigger and more difficult to solve. We accomplish nothing until we find *answers*. Grousing about problems is easier than doing something about them. As we have exposed the problems in previous chapters, our goal has been understanding God's ways of solving them. Easy to conceive and hard to achieve! Unless we tap into the divine power point, that's the way it will stay. He who has given us the indwelling Spirit also gives us grace to help in time of need.[1] Here's the point: we head-off most of the problems facing us and solve the rest by being God's people and doing what He *told* us to do.

Doing is difficult because *honesty* is difficult. We are like the fat, middle-aged person who looks in the mirror and sees someone young and athletic. Taking a thorough and analytical look at Jesus and his apostles comes first. Then we must have the honesty to ask, "Why have we failed to proceed in the direction they pointed?"

Somewhere, somehow, we took a fork in the road Jesus never intended us to travel. Certainly he didn't travel it himself. Consequently, we are either bogged down or going the wrong direction. Choosing the wrong fork has caused us to bog down in building bigger, fancier buildings. The wrong direction has led us fill them with people from other churches and call it "success". What direction does Jesus want us to take? The answer is in Matthew, Mark, Luke and John.

Most of us find *determining* the right direction much easier than actually *taking* it. Being a counter-culture, going against the flow of humanism in our age, requires clear vision and solid determination. Such a stand will bring us ridicule and ostracism. The elite of our age will disdainfully dismiss us as hopelessly naive and archaic. Only those whose hearts are receptive will recognize the road to life when they see it.

If the heartaches and troubles of the world have pried your heart open, be forewarned! Involvement in the lives and salvation of human beings is fraught with deprivation and pain. No longer can your life be yours alone. No longer can you avoid the suffering and pain of others. As the Master who walked before us, we are here for the world. A line from his *Liverpool Oratorio* reveals how Paul McCartney has come to view himself in the course of human events: *"Not for ourselves but for the whole world were we born, / And we were born in Liverpool."* He goes on to observe, *"Being born where you were born, / Carries with it certain responsibilities."*[2]

How true of those born into the family of God!

Citizens of Zion, born for the whole world, have certain responsibilities. Those who understand this have taken up the cross of Jesus and are honored to bear it daily.

We children of God must individually and collectively recapture the mission given us by Jesus. Shaking-off distractions, we must concentrate on precisely who we are and for what we are truly responsible. God's Word records the definitions and directives we need. It's time we took a look!

Ten Practical Steps To Revolution

These suggestions sum up the previous chapters. I hope they will encourage you in your plans to share Christ with your world.

1. Study Jesus. Notice his purpose, priorities, motivation, message and methods.

2. Study the apostles of Jesus. Notice their emphases. Notice how they spent their time and energy.

3. Determine to make these characteristics yours.

4. Like Jesus and his apostles, pray for the wisdom, discernment, power and resources God has promised to give us unlimited amounts.

5. Be convicted of the lost condition of those outside of the kingdom as were Jesus and the apostles.

6. Like Jesus and the apostles, make genuine friends of those outside the kingdom. Eat, work, and play with them. Be involved in their lives.

7. Gain credibility through good works of mercy and kindness, especially in times of crisis as did Jesus and the apostles.

8. Become involved in the organizations and power structures of your community in order to exert Christian influence as the church of the New Testament did.

9. Envision and work for a victorious church that

glorifies God, exalts Christ, saves souls, and makes disciples. Be involved in the programs and ministries of the church.

10. Envision and work for a church that functions as the body, with all the members fulfilling their necessary functions, using their God-given talents, gifts, abilities, and encouraging others to do so.

These are the absolute necessities of the Urgent Revolution. We have a long way to go. Let's get busy!

A PROPOSAL

When I returned from our 1991 trip to Adelaide, South Australia, I began to discuss with my church elders the possibility of working with them in this fast-growing area of the Dallas/Ft. Worth Metroplex. I had already scheduled another visit to Australia. They graciously allowed me to keep that appointment.

These two trips gave me a renewed and fresh perspective. They confirmed that if we do not treat our "local" works just like our "mission" efforts, we shall fail to fulfill our commission.

Just previous to my second trip, I left a document with the elders, called simply, "A Proposal." I asked myself the question: *"If we approached the work in our community as we would any other mission field, what changes and adjustments would we make?*

As I wrote, I tried to be scriptural — determined *not* to be restricted by *custom* or the *tradition*. I wanted to look at my community as I would any other mission point, with two concerns *only*: (1) reaching the lost with the gospel and (2) edifying and equipping the faithful. I would not concern myself with preserving "the way we've always done it," or, "where it might lead," but only with "what is the *best way* to do it?"

If we were asked to begin a "mission effort" in our area, what would we do? What changes would we make in order to maximize the use of our time, energy and talents? What would be necessary to become a congregation geared to reach the lost and establish their faith?

I believe it is possible to become a powerful force for preaching the gospel and reaping the harvest in any community. I am not the final authority on everything that can and should be done, but this proposal was my response to the need to put my congregation on an evangelistic footing. I feel as much effort needs to be expended in seeking and saving the lost as edifying and equipping the saints. This will be done by restructuring our use of time and energy.

The ideas put forth here are not fully developed, even in my own mind. These are concepts evangelists and elders must develop together. Elders and staff, working together must fully discuss, develop, implement or discard them. Here is what I suggested for the Grapevine church. I hope this stimulates thinking and discussion.

1. EVANGELISTIC INVOLVEMENT BY MEMBERS: The ingredient most effective in outreach. Members will be encouraged to practice "friendship evangelism" by cultivating friendships with non-Christians.[3] The purpose is finding opportunities to communicate the gospel in natural ways. There is a great deal of material available to help our families learn how to do this effectively. As leaders, we will set goals to be met by families and individuals. Their achievements in this area must then be recognized and applauded.

2. VISIBILITY: We will make efforts to increase the

public profile of the church (including the media, see No. 6).

a. Public, well-advertised projects: painting & repairing houses, repairing autos, clean-up campaigns, a victory garden to feed the hungry, quilting bees, etc.

b. Public events sponsored by the church in public venues such as popular singing groups (New Creation, ACappella, etc.), talent shows, musicals, plays, and other events that utilize the artistic gifts of our members

c. Fund-raisers for various service areas and community needs (pancake suppers, bake sales, yard sales, car washes, benefits).

d. Adequate Signage.

e. Awareness of our existence (which I believe is low, especially among newcomers) achieved by distributing a brochure addressing needs indicated by demographic studies. It is very beneficial to consult with members in the field of advertising.

f. We will consider better utilization of our present facilities. We need to turn our under-used auditorium into a multipurpose room. I'm suggesting basketball goals...the lot. It will greatly increase our seating capacity. The area can then be used as an evangelistic tool; particularly for our youth. We can make it look as good as or better than it does now and many times more useful.

3. ASSEMBLIES: We are currently enjoying excellent attendance at both Sunday AM and PM assemblies. However, we need to face the reality that very few churches have over 50% of their Sunday morning

attendees back for Sunday evening. Therefore, I suggest:

a. Bible Classes 9 - 10 a.m.

b. Break for refreshments 10 - 10:30

c. Sunday Morning assembly 10:30 - 12 p.m.

d. Lunch for all who wish to stay 12 - 1:00 p.m., perhaps ending with a devotional.

e. Sunday Evening assembly, as we presently know it, will be eliminated in favor of small groups and ministry meetings with one exception discussed below.

4. SMALL GROUPS meeting in member's homes will be one focus of Sunday evening. Elders and evangelists will "fan-out" with their families to meet with various groups. Format and curriculum will be prepared by elders, evangelists and teachers after researching successful methods elsewhere. Evangelist and elders will act as resource persons in doctrinal concerns. A traditional assembly must be held for those whose work schedule keeps them from attending the main assembly.

5. WEDNESDAY EVENING will be structured to equip the saints on various levels. There will be a "Basics of Christianity" class for new Christians and others who need it. This could be the time for training classes for young men and women.

6. MEDIA OUTREACH: Staff will be responsible for:

a. Bulletin — needs to be very sharp and attractive. It should be sent to anyone who is a member or attends. It will convey the image we want to project.

b. Newspaper — a regular teaching article.

c. Television & Radio programs and advertising.

d. Writing, publishing brochures, tracts, books, etc.

7. FACILITIES: We will give special attention to building and grounds, reception areas, foyer, auditorium and classrooms. We will utilize the gifts of members who are professional designers to assure these areas look attractive, warm, and inviting to visitors.

8. NEW CONVERTS will be assigned to mature Christian families who are responsible for further nurturing. Their responsibilities will include:

a. Orientation

b. Continuing studies to nurture and ground them in the faith. Curriculum can be provided and guidance given.

c. Introduction into a small group if they are not already in one.

d. Assisting them to fill-out their "Inventory of Gifts" form and returning it to the office.

e. This process needs periodic checking. Those new converts who choose not to participate would not be involved in ministries until they do.

9. NEW MEMBERS BY TRANSFER: Keep a list of members who have transferred to us within the last six months. A checklist, or something similar, is used to assure assimilation into congregational life.

10. CHRISTIAN PRESCHOOL, was originally begun as an outreach program. It has been responsible for

several conversions and must continue in its original purpose.

11. PLANNING SESSIONS: Elders and evangelists will be involved in regular prayer, study, creative thinking. They should constantly evaluate the progress of evangelism and edification.

It is important that staff and members understand involvement in *everything* is impossible. Families should be allot time for the enhancement of family life.

To have people in homes to share the gospel is an example of Christianity in action. Our children are greatly helped by this. However, a family hosting a small group (in addition to supporting other efforts) will not have time and energy left for other major ministries. Everyone should seek to serve in the areas best suited for his / her talents and abilities. We must discern who is gifted to preach and give them opportunities to address the flock. In addition to this being our scriptural obligation (to allow the exercise of these gifts), it will also free up more of the evangelists' time for work in achieving the above goals.

Thinking realistically, perhaps we should not expect to see revolutionary changes quickly made within older, established churches. As new congregations are begun, these ideas can be put to good use. Most of these principles can be applied anywhere. Actually, if we expect to see much happen, they *must* be. No church, old or young, will implement all of the suggestions in the proposal as envisioned. It is vital, however, *something* be done. We can accomplish his will by multitudes of alternative methods. If we are *moving forward* I say, "Hallelujah!". If goals are clarified and thinking stimulated, something very important is taking place. Truitt Adair writes,

> The bottom line is: regardless of whether we meet in a stained-glass building, a gymnasium, or in a grass hut — regardless of whether we meet on Sunday A.M., P.M., — both — or all day; we are likely to grow if we get two things right: (1) Agressive pursuit of the lost. (2) Intensive training of the members for service. Without these essentials, all the fine tuning in the world is for naught.[4]

Thousands of practical ways exist for refocusing our efforts toward reaching the lost and unchurched. Spending time and energy "brainstorming" will surface creative and effective ways to involve every member young and old. Every move toward aggressive participation in the community lends further credibility to the gospel we preach.

How I Do It

Let me depart from being practical for a moment and get emotional. No feeling in this world compares with the rush of sharing Jesus with another human being. It is a "high" better felt than told. It is a "buzz" not found in any earthly drug. What happens within when you share your personal story of salvation? What is it that stirs the spirit so? I struggle to find adequate words to describe it.

No doubt God could reach the world without our puny human participation. That he has allowed us in on the action has to be another proof of his love. I believe he allows us to participate *because of the good it does us!*

Evangelism is the lifeblood of the church. To

evangelize is to participate in the convicting work of the Spirit. We can get no closer than this to the blood of Christ. Evangelism is to see the death, burial and resurrection of Christ over and
over as the hopeless dead are given rebirth and new life.

There is another blessing that comes from sharing Jesus I have not touched on. As I left Australia for a furlough to the States back in the seventies, one of our new Christians, Eileen Tomes, handed me a note and instructed me not to read it until our ship was out to sea.

After all the tearful goodbyes, I sat down on the bed in our cabin and tore open the envelope. As long as I live, I shall never forget the contents of that note. It was only one sentence long but it filled my heart like a million words. It sums up for me one of the greatest thrills of outreach, the thrill of realizing God has used you to bring people to him who are searching and groping in the darkness to fill an emptiness in their life. The note simply read, "Thank you, Dwight, for knocking on our door."

Eileen has gone on before us now; her battle over, her race completed. Standing between me (a vessel for the message of salvation) and Eileen (one seeking salvation), was a barrier to all of heaven's blessings of less than two inches of wood. God gave me the courage to knock on that door, and Eileen opened it. I did not teach her family, I simply set up the date and time for one of my co-workers to come and share the gospel with them. But someone had to knock on the door.

Her husband, Len, eventually became a leader in the congregation.   Their children have become pillars of the church in other places. When I think about the Tomes family and my participation in their salvation, do I have a good feeling? Wow! If only I could describe how good it is! God wants you to have this feeling too.

If you pray for God to lead you to seeking souls, each

person you meet on a daily basis is a potential answer to prayer. This way of looking at people has not come naturally to me; it is something cultivated for many years. And so, I try to leave a good impression with everyone (not easy in rush-hour traffic!).

A non-believer will only meet Jesus through those God fills with his Spirit. That means I am the person of Jesus to the one who works on my car, checks out my groceries, sells me something or buys something from me. My neighbor will have contact with Jesus only through me, so my greeting should be friendly. My dealings should be honest and courteous. My interest and concern should be genuine and not motivated by a desire to put another "conversion notch" in my Bible.

One of the editors reviewing this manuscript wrote in the margin of the above paragraph, "How is this revolutionary? Seems rather commonplace to me." I only wish she was right! Truly, it *ought* to seem commonplace to us all, but as researcher George Barna reports, only 50% of Evangelicals and 38% of "Born-again Christians" think of themselves as ambassadors of Jesus Christ. He concludes:

> Most committed Christians fail to con-
> sistently view themselves as His repre-
> sentatives. Perhaps recognizing that we
> are both called to be His reflection in
> this world, and that the world watches
> us more closely than we may realize,
> will better enable us to shape our think-
> ing and behavior to confirm to His call-
> ing on our lives.[5]

I may never be able to reach my mechanic or see my neighbor come to Jesus. That bothers me, not because I feel I've failed, but because they may be eternally lost. I am simply an "opportunity-giver." I can plant, you can water, but only God can cause growth.[6]

But how do I know if people honestly show an interest in Jesus? Although you can never really know about the honesty, if they ask you about Jesus or your faith or hope, you can be sure they are giving you an opportunity. Notice the methods of Jesus. In the vast majority of cases, Jesus *did not initiate the spiritual dialogue...others* did. They began the conversation:

> *"Teacher, I will follow you wherever You go."(Matthew 8:19)*
> *"Why does your teacher eat with tax-collectors and 'sinners'?" (9:11)*
> *"Look! Your disciples are doing what is unlawful on the Sabbath." (12:2)*
> *"Teacher, we want to see a miraculous sign from you."(12:38)*
> *"Why do your disciples break the tradition of the elders?" (15:12)*
> *"By what authority are you doing these things?" they asked. "And who gave you authority to do this?"(Mark 11:28)*
> *"Teacher, we know you are a man of integrity. You aren't swayed by men, because you pay no attention to who they are; but you teach the way of God in accordance with the truth. Is it right to pay taxes to Caesar or not? Should we pay or shouldn't we?"(Mark 12:14, 15)*
> *"Rabbi, we know you are a teacher who has come from God. For no one could perform the miraculous signs you are doing if God were not with him." (John 3:2)*

We could multiply examples such as this. As we

conduct ourselves as Christian men and women in our world, it will be the same with us. Because of some kindness, some act of mercy, some good deed, some gracious word, we will proclaim the Word of God. "Why are you doing this?" "Why are you different?" "Why are you so kind?" "You're one of those religious fanatics." "Christianity is for sissies, women and children." Hundreds of possible leading questions or statements can open the door for the gospel.

Leroy Brownlow tells a story that illustrates this so well!

> During the Korean War a chaplain saw a severely wounded soldier lying on the field of battle. Wanting to minister to him, he inquired, "Would you like for me to read some strengthening passages from the Bible?"
>
> "Right now I had rather have a drink. I'm dying of thirst," was the reply.
>
> And away rushed the chaplain who soon returned with water to quench the fallen soldier's thirst. Then he took off his scarf, rolled it into a little pillow, and placed it under the soldier's head.
>
> "I'm so cold," mumbled the badly wounded soldier.
>
> On hearing this, the chaplain removed his top coat and spread it over the ill man.
>
> "Now," whispered the attended soldier, "if there's anything in that book that makes you so kind, read it to me please."[7]

Christian conduct may provide you with an opportunity to invite inquisitive people into your home or to your prayer/study group. The time may come when you can say,

"Jennifer, would you like to sit down and talk with me about Jesus/Christianity sometime? Can you come over for dinner/coffee/dessert/lunch Friday night? Can I buy your lunch tomorrow? Perhaps we can talk about these matters then." If she accepts this invitation, you have a wonderful opportunity to (a) get to know her better and possibly (b) become involved in a discussion about Jesus.

If Jennifer wants to talk about Christianity, you might begin by saying something like: "Jenny, a friend of mine and I were studying the Bible one time, and she helped me to see all people, including me, are sinners." At that point, you can share a couple of passages, such as Romans 3:9,10, 23 and 1 John 1:8-10. "I came to see even *one sin* could keep a person out of heaven and I could never live a life good enough to *earn* my salvation. Then my friend helped me to see that only because of the sacrifice of Jesus on the cross could I be forgiven of all my sins, past, present and future, and make it to heaven." At each point, have her read some passages plainly teaching this. Talk about God's love and grace.

If she asks the age-old question, "What must I do to be saved?" you can then share the word of God with her about accepting God's grace through repentance, faith, and baptism.

After spending a lot of time trying to win souls I can tell you each case is different. The only way to develop a comfortable approach is through *experience*. The *gospel* is the power for salvation, not *our* words. Really trusting the power of the gospel, we confidently, yet gently, place it into open hearts and let it do its work. It is wondrous to behold!

There are probably as many techniques for making a *practical* effort to reach our communities as there are churches. However, we don't need more *methods*. We need more motivation! Jesus has left the how up to us. But he has not left the what up to us. We need to stop here, close this book, fall to our knees and ask directions to the nearest open heart, then pour the love of Jesus into it.

[1]Hebrews 4:15,16

[2]Paul McCartney, *Liverpool Oratorio,* MPL Communications Ltd, 1992, pp 32,33

[3] This is certainly not the only method. In the gospels and Acts, we see many natural ways of reaching people with the gospel.

[4]Truitt Adair, Director of Sunset International Bible Institute, editorial comment

[5]George Barna, *Absolute Confusion,* Regal Books, a division of Gospel Light, Ventura, CA 93006, 1993, pp. 49, 57

[6]I Corinthians 3:5-7

[7]Leroy Brownlow, *The Fruit of the Spirit,* Brownlow Publishing Company, 1989, 6309 Airport Freeway, Fort Worth, TX 76117, pp. 55,56

12

REVOLUTIONARY PRAYER

To Pray Like Jesus

*Yet the news about him spread all the
more, so that crowds of people came to
hear him and to be healed of their sick-
nesses. But Jesus often withdrew to
lonely places and prayed.[1]*

Jesus would have been a bust as a babyboomer. He
sought the loneliness of a starlit mountainside to pray even
though there were people to heal, places to go, things to do,
sermons to preach. He left the clamoring crowds behind to
refill his spiritual reservoir in places of solitude and he didn't
even take a beeper or cellular phone!

*Very early in the morning, while it was
still dark, Jesus got up, left the house
and went off to a solitary place, where
he prayed. Simon and his companions
went to look for him, and when they
found him, they exclaimed: "Everyone
is looking for you!"[2]*

The mandate of his mission and the countdown of the cross compelled Jesus to preach and do miraculous works in villages and towns...one after another. The tyranny of the multitudes, begging him to meet their physical needs, constantly tugged at his compassionate heart. Jesus, however, knowing the water of life cannot be drawn from empty buckets, sought solitude and the in-flight refueling of prayer.

Of all we understand and employ about following Christ, we do the poorest job regarding prayer. When we discuss our habits and customs of prayer, most of us shamefully confess our poverty. Indeed, the difference between Jesus' and the apostles approach to prayer and ours leaps from our Bibles.

Our culture considers withdrawal to a lonely place *unproductive,* a vacation. Waking moments not filled with some kind of frenzied activity is an alien concept. We lament the lack of power in our walk and calmness in our lifestyle. Yet, we spend minuscule amounts of time in places where God can empower our lives and pour the oil of peace on the troubled waters of our mind.

Intensity

> One of those days Jesus went out to a mountainside to pray and spent the night praying to God. When morning came, he called his disciples to him and chose twelve of them, whom he also designated apostles.[3]

He spent the night praying! Think of it! A prayer longer than sixty seconds! We are too busy, too distracted, too unfocused to schedule a few minutes to pray, much less a *whole night!* Luke notes this lengthy, intense time of prayer, without sensation, comment, or fanfare. Why? Because to Luke it seemed *normal* to pray seriously, fervently, and at length. When the wide-eyed disciples returned to the upper room after witnessing the ascension of Jesus, *"They all joined together constantly in prayer, along with the women and Mary the mother of Jesus, and with his brothers."[4]*

After Pentecost, Luke describes the disciples in Jerusalem: *"They devoted themselves to the apostles' teaching and to fellowship, to the breaking of bread and to prayer."[5]* The amount of attention given it by the Holy Spirit, indicates the essential nature of frequent, thankful, fervent, intercessory, dependent, prayer. Paul exhorts the Romans, *"Be...faithful in prayer."[6]* He urges the church at Colossae, *"Devote yourselves to prayer."[7]* He advises the Thessalonians to *"Pray continually."[8]* Regrettably, words of Scripture and reality often live miles apart.

More than important, prayer is *indispensable!* By it we connect to God's power, His leading. Norman Vincent Peale wrote,

> "Prayer, someone has said, is not overcoming God's reluctance; it is laying hold on His highest willingness. Certainly it is the simplest and most effective way of making contact with the Power that orders the spinning galaxies and yet watches the sparrow's fall."

The disciples were "devoted" to prayer. In the Greek, the word means "strong, stanch," and carries the idea of "steady persistence." The verb means "to persist obstinately in." They gave themselves to teaching, fellowship, and prayer. They knew prayer is not boxed up and opened only during "quiet times" or "devotionals,"[9] not as a duty to be discharged but a privilege to be enjoyed. While large blocks of time given to prayer are good and proper, ongoing prayer is even better. Prayer as second nature is our goal.

Begun upon waking, continued while dressing, eating breakfast, commuting to work, strolling down the street, shopping for groceries, between classes, watching the news, taking a shower, walking the dog, it becomes as natural as breathing. I like the way Robert Fulghum, speaking of the routine tasks of life, put it.

> ...as often is not, we use these times to reflect and talk to ourselves.

> Or meditate — even pray.

> Just because you aren't on your knees in church or sitting still in a cramped position doesn't mean you can't be talking to God. Just because both you and God are busy doesn't mean you can't be in touch.

> Such times are the sacred part of the secret life.

> Such times keep my soul sane.[10]

A word to my fellow preachers, invite the Holy Spirit into your study. Prayer marshals all the forces of heaven in our work of seeking, saving, reproving, rebuking, exhorting, equipping, comforting, establishing, teaching, and encouraging. What we labor to deliver in our pulpits must first be conceived on our knees and gestated in the womb of the word. If you are a teacher, deacon, elder or involved in any ministry, let prayer guide and empower your work.

Labor

Remember Anna in the temple? "She never left the temple but worshiped night and day, fasting and praying."[11] "Epaphras," said Paul to Colossae, "is always wrestling in prayer for you."[12] He urged the Roman Christians to "Join me in my struggle by praying to God for me."[13] Jesus, on his face in the dirt and rocks of Gethsemane, did the sweaty work of prayer. Wrestling, struggling, sweating...prayer is *toil,* a ministry of hard work.

Prayer is an act of willful obedience; not mood or inclination. Oswald Chambers said, "Prayer is not just an exercise routine God has us on; it's our business...Prayer is our holy occupation. Pure and simple."[14] Spiritually complete Christians may spend much time in prayer, but most of us identify with C.S. Lewis who wrote, "If we were perfected, prayer would not be a duty, it would be a delight."

Prayer as *hard work* is a revelation to us. No longer should we scold ourselves for being in no mood to pray. We no longer need to feel guilty when getting on our knees becomes onerous. We must pray as we love: in obedience to the wishes of our Father in Heaven, in season, out of season, with perseverance, steadfastly, unconditionally. Sometimes prayer comes easily, a sweet communion. Sometimes it is just plain *hard.*

Preparation

As the sun rose above the Galilean hills, Jesus rose from a night of prayer. There was good reason for such intensive, extended prayer. It was time to choose twelve men to comprise his "inner circle." He would never take such a significant step in his ministry without securing spiritual support from his Father. Refilled and equipped, the selection process began.

Out of the hundreds that followed him, these would be the ones who, in a few short years, would chop, toss and mix the Caesar salad of the Roman Empire and turn the world upside down! As they filled the world with his message, their words carried the same authority as his. Did he spend the night going over their resumes? Did he call them in for a second interview? No, he was about something far more important and effective. A quick mini-prayer at bedtime would not suffice. A hasty request added to the meal-time blessing would never do. This motley collection of fishermen, a politician, and a tax collector had been the subject of hours of prayer...in solitude...on a mountainside.

On these twelve men, hinged the salvation of millions. They were men of action and not particularly analytic. They were probably unaware that their activity would not only liberate those of their day enslaved to sin, but also those of two millennia later! One thing they surely understood: their job was to preach and pray. When administrative matters threatened to hinder their ability to *"give...attention to prayer and the ministry of the word,"* they made adjustments necessary to remove the distraction and stay on course.[15] Not only did this please *"the whole group,"* but a "gospel explosion" resulted. *"So the word of God spread. The number of disciples in Jerusalem increased rapidly, and a large number of priests became obedient to the faith."*[16]

Prayer is pivotal to the liberation of the cause of Christ. We give amazing amounts of time, energy, and attention to *methods*. There's nothing wrong with methods; but neglecting that which empowers any method is senseless!

The connection between the cause of Christ and prayer is mysterious. It goes beyond logical analysis. We pray, expecting an answer without knowing the "how." It is enough to know that prayer and ministry of the word are wed in holy matrimony. Divorce is impossible. One cannot function properly without the other. What God has joined together let not man put asunder.

Power

> *"They all joined together constantly in prayer, along with the women and Mary the mother of Jesus, and with his brothers"*[17]

Central to the Urgent Revolution is a prayer revolution. We must think of prayer as the plug that taps into God as power outlet. The first Christians, taking their cue from Jesus and his messengers, prayed before, during, and after significant events recorded in Acts and the Letters. It is safe to conclude that no work was ever undertaken without a preceding session of fervent prayer. Often, prayer was combined with fasting. When they sent out Barnabas and Paul, they prayed first. *"While they were worshipping the Lord and fasting, the Holy Spirit said, "Set apart for me Barnabas and Saul for the work to which I have called them." So after they had fasted and prayed, they placed their hands on them and sent them off."*[18]

On that journey, they appointed shepherds for the churches but again, not without prayer and fasting. *"Paul and Barnabas appointed elders for them in each church and, with prayer and fasting, committed them to the Lord, in whom they had put their trust."*[19] Oswald Chambers wrote,

> "We tend to use prayer as a last resort, but Jesus wants it to be our first line of defense. We pray when there's nothing else we can do, but Jesus wants us to pray before we do anything at all."[20]

If we want to recapture the revolutionary spirit of the Body of Christ, we must recapture the power only prayer can bring.

Notice the power-link? Bold proclamation comes when we plug into prayer. When the Sanhedrin warned Peter and John to *"speak no longer to anyone in this name,"* they stood their holy ground. *"For we cannot help speaking about what we have seen and heard."*[21] When they reported all this to the church, the first item on the agenda was to pray. They *"raised their voices together in prayer to God."* Look at the awesome result:

> *"After they prayed, the place where they were meeting was shaken. And they were all filled with the Holy Spirit and spoke the word of God boldly With great power the apostles continued to testify to the resurrection of the Lord Jesus, and much grace was upon them all."*[22]

God give us praying, shaking, spirit-filled churches! Only then will we boldly proclaim the word of God to a starving, expectant world.

No doubt we preachers need to spend less time berating God's people and more time praying for them! Jesus did![23] Paul did![24] He even urged Christians to pray for each other![25] When God's people really connect with Him, our church buildings and assembly halls will vibrate in holy resonance to the moving of the Spirit!

Do we want the *"message of the Lord"* to *"spread rapidly and be honored"*?[26] Pray! Do we want to *"Fearlessly make known the mystery of the gospel"* to *"declare it fearlessly as (we) should"*?[27] Pray! Do we desire *"the way be opened"*?[28] Pray! The most powerful and gifted proclaimer still needs brethren joining his struggle by praying for him.[29]

The Warriors

Try to tell a certain group of women I call "The Warriors" that prayer doesn't work! Lorie Skaggs, Conna Sullivan, Rena Velasquez, and Valerie Frazier have *seen* it work. Not only do they believe what the Bible teaches about prayer, they *practice* it. Lorie has been a Christian for two years. Excited about her faith, she immediately began reaching out to her friends. In these first two years she has been primarily responsible for eight conversions! For Lorie, however, there are simply never enough people to teach! Recently, when she felt her ministry was dragging a bit, she began to pray with the warriors for more opportunities. Amazing things began to happen! People emerged from strange places.

Lorie is happily married to Jody, her first conversion! Forced to maintain contact with the father of her daughter from a previous marriage, she became acquainted with Connie, his fiancee. When Connnie also experienced difficulties, she inexplicably turned to Lorie. Lorie knew exactly where to get help for Connie — God's word. Following weeks of intense study and much support from The Warriors, a very excited Connie McAfee was immersed into Christ. Accidental? Coincidental? The Warriors would not agree.

Recently, another bizarre incident occurred when a very upset neighbor confronted Lori. The neighbor's husband had left her. Already suspicious that Lori, might have had something to do with it, she decided to confront her. The more Lorie listened, the more she realized this must be another seeking soul sent by the Spirit. That very day she spent three hours in the word with this erstwhile enemy! Again, The Warriors, now including Connie, convened to struggle in prayer for her conversion. It is hard to describe the rejoicing as, a few weeks later, Kim Adamson was born again. Prayer, one of the most powerful tools God places in the hands of his people, lies neglected in the bottom of our spiritual toolbox. In contrast, our spiritual ancestors seldom put it down. Kneeling on beaches, lifting holy hands in assemblies, raising prayerful petitions for a jailed comrade, seeking boldness for an apostle on the front lines, healing for the sick, forgiveness for the sinner, progress for the gospel, strength for the weak, wisdom for the rulers — their prayers grace the pages of our Bibles.

Recapturing The Dynamic

Horrified, we watch our fellow soldiers, haplessly marching behind blind leaders, wander into a dark and dangerous swamp and become bogged in the quicksand of pride and the mud of apathy. Forward motion ceases as they vainly struggle to free themselves from the brown, viscous muck.

How could such disaster overtake the most powerful army ever fielded? How do we extract God's army from this muck and get back on the front lines? The answer: *We* don't!

We get into these messes by depending on ourselves: our wisdom, our resources, our direction. We ignore the map God gives us, lose contact with our heavenly headquarters and find ourselves stuck in the goo of consequence. We will get out of it by getting on our knees and restoring contact with headquarters. Following commands, and depending on God's power, we will pull ourselves from the clinging filth of the mud. We will wash and purify ourselves, consult the divine map and the holy compass. Then we will get back on course. From now on, we will *maintain* communication with our Commander.

He was always there, observing us from a heavenly perspective. He saw his misguided forces wandering aimlessly, led by prideful field officers, closing in on the dangerous, dismal swamp. Perhaps he wondered, "Why do they fail to keep in touch? Why do they ignore the map I provided for them?" The indwelling Spirit, the ministering angels — all in vain for an army that does not pray!

Do we want to recapture the dynamic of the first Christians as they exploded into their world with the gospel? Do we covet their power? Do we desire their single-minded devotion? Then we must learn to pray as they did: fervently, earnestly, humbly, frequently, thankfully, striving, struggling, laboring, pleading, interceding. You see, they were disciples of Jesus — ordinary people who desired to be like Him. To *pray* like Jesus.

[1]Luke 5:15,16

[2]Mark 1:35-37

[3]Luke 6:12,13

[4]Acts 1:14

[5]Acts 2:42

[6]Romans 12:12

[7]Colossians 4:2

[8]1 Thessalonians 5:17

[9]Our modern use of the word, "devotional", illustrates how some modern catch-phrases are not found in Scripture and, when they are, we have managed to change their meaning into something quite different.

[10]Robert Fulghum, *Maybe (Maybe Not)*, Ivy Books, Published by Ballantine Books, New York, 1995, p. 31

[11]Luke 2:37

[12]Colossians 4:12

[13]Romans 15:30

[14]Oswald Chambers, introduction to *Prayer: A Holy Occupation,* Copyright 1992 by Oswald Chambers Publications Association, Limited, Discovery House, Nashville, Tennessee 37214, p.8

[15]Acts 6:3,4

[16]Acts 6:7

[17]Acts 1:14

[18]Acts 13:2,3

[19]Acts 14:23

[20]Oswald Chambers, introduction to *Prayer: A Holy Occupation,* p.7

[21]Acts 4:20

[22]Acts 4:31 and 33

[23]John 17:18,20

[24]Colossians 1:9,10

[25]Ephesians 6:18

[26]2 Thessalonians 3:1

[27]Ephesians 6:19,20

[28]Romans 1:10

[29]Romans 15:30.

13

THE CHANGE AGENTS

The Mandate

Blue-coifed Mrs. Jane Barrington had never been outside her home state before. But when her husband passed away, her children thought a trip to Europe would help the process of grief recovery. Joining a tour made of others of her vintage, Mrs. Barrington actually began to see the places mentioned in her school history books. The tour visited many places in many cities, including towering cathedrals filled with treasure, art and history. It was all so very wonderful, but something began to nag at her, especially in the cathedrals and historic church buildings. Finally, at the end of the umpteenth lecture in the umpteenth sanctuary, Mrs. Jane could stand it no longer. When the guide asked for questions she mustered her courage. In her tiny, shy voice she said, "The cathedral is indeed beautiful and its history is all very interesting, but has anybody been saved here lately?" I heard the story years ago. Variations arise every now and then, but the message remains the same: saving souls is more important than anything else.

We enjoy hunting shells on the beach. Looking at the beautiful shapes and colors, we easily forget they once housed a living animal. They die, their home erodes into sand, or becomes a curiosity admired by passers-by. Similarly, the cathedrals of Europe exist today as shrines to the tourist trade. Historically, they were the core of life: centers of learning, sources of morality, crowded with worshippers. Today, tourists fill them. They admire them as monuments, not to God, but to architecture and artistic achievement. They endure as part of the tattered tapestry of medieval and renaissance life.

While many would like to see a return to the "glory days" when cathedrals were the focal point of European cities and villages, this appears unlikely. To the European, cathedrals represent all that is *wrong* with religion. The religion of the cathedrals stubbornly refused to stay relevant to the relentlessly changing world around them.

As the Bible became available, Roman Catholicism decreed it "forbidden." As scientists of the day discovered the nature of the universe and the way our bodies work, the Roman church treated them as heretics. Its response to challenges of cherished myths and traditions was inquisition, punishment, torture and death. The popes declared themselves infallible. The clergy assumed dictatorial powers. To doubt or question the teachings and authority of the church was blasphemy. Sinners paid for their transgressions with the indulgences which paid for many of the cathedrals. Then the reformers, sick of smelling the stench of corruption, arose in wrathful indignation. The solid base of Roman Catholicism began to erode. Today, empty cathedrals echo with silent testimony: the church stays *relevant* or it *dies*.

Change is imperative! Not simply for the sake of change, but for the sake of *relevance*. In his landmark study, *Megatrends,* John Naisbitt points to the railroads as an example of stubborn irrelevance.

> The great business lesson of unrecognized obsolescence is not buggy whips, it's the railroads. Suppose that somewhere along the way a railroad company, sensing the changes its business environment, had engaged in the process of reconceptualizing what business it was in. Suppose they had said, "Let's get out of the railroad business and into the transportation business." They could have created systems that moved goods by rail, truck, airplane, or in combination, as appropriate. "Moved goods" is the customer-oriented point. Instead, they continued to be transfixed by the lore of railroading that had served the country so well—until the world changed.[1]

The world *has* changed. Culture has also changed. The essence of the gospel remains wonderfully relevant because man's basic nature has *not* changed. Our sins have not, in essence, changed. The church, however, faced with the necessity of relating to modern human beings, is paraplegic. We are too weak to competently get the gospel to our changed world or influence our changed culture. As Leith Anderson points out,

> Renewal is not something we do at periodic intervals. The best organizations are always renewing. They are always going through a process of change in which they throw out the worst and retain the best. This sorting out process guarantees both stability and relevance.[2]

Again, Naisbitt concurs,

> The trick, of course, is to be alert to changes around you, to anticipate their impact on your institution, and then to respond: to reconceptualize what you are up to. Disastrous results tell us something is very wrong. But we ought to be able to hear the signals before they get quite so strong.

> The work process should be emphasized. What I am talking about is not a product you get or buy from the outside. It is something that occurs inside an institution (well instructed by what is going on outside). It is the hard work of colleagues rigorously questioning every aspect of an institution's purpose — and the questioning of the purpose itself. The purpose must be right, and must be a shared vision, a strategic vision.[3]

What can we do to *change?* In this case, change will mean restoring the *direction* of the church. It will mean focusing on *people* and *purpose* more than process. It will mean passionately pursuing the leading of that first band of empowered disciples. The love of Jesus summons us to rally around the same cause, follow the same Master, tap into the same surging power, feel the same insistent urgings, enjoy the same God-glorifying results.

Our churches seek refuge in the eye of a hurricane called "Change." But such refuge can't last in the rapidly moving storm. Change swirls around us threatening to engulf us in high tides and tornadic winds. No longer do the years drift by without much difference. Constant change continually thrusts itself upon us, forcing us to move faster and faster. Those born since World War II cannot remember it being any other way. The flood of new information, technology, and entertainment options speeds after us down the information superhighway. We either move with it, or...thump-thump!

Major changes in religion and philosophy challenge entrenched traditions. As Donald Posterski has written:

> The religious profile of North America used to be monolithic. Increased ethnicity, the arrival of representatives from other world religions and experimentation with other supernatural alternatives, such as the New Age movement, are altering our religious profile.[4]

Five hundred years ago, the printing press revolutionized the world. Today, the electronic media and computer age spark an even greater revolution. The science fiction of my youth becomes the non-fiction of my adulthood. New spinoffs from these technologies come thick and fast. Accurate predictions of these drastic and unimaginable changes are impossible.

Before our eyes, a global economy forces the nations of the world to interdependence. Shifting populations and rapidly growing ethnic groups confront us. In Western countries these days, both parents work and depend on institutionalized child-care to look after the kids. The morass of drugs, racism and immorality bogs us down. Homosexuals openly parade their perversion and clamor for protective legislation. We struggle with euthanasia for the suffering and terminally ill. Surrogate mothers bear children for a price. Abortion continues as the birth-control choice of millions. Other problems come up like weeds to challenge mores planted and established centuries ago, yet the church stagnates in the dried-up riverbed of the forties and fifties as the world sweeps by in new channels.

In our church was a sweet lady in her nineties who has now passed on to her reward. Even at that advanced age she was alert, intelligent[5] and regular in attendance. When I think of the changes she witnessed, I had to admire her ability to think clearly! In her time the church and town went through major transitions. Her faith and service, however, remained strong.

Given the rapid and substantial changes in our world, we must *also* remain strong and faithful. And yet, *we must change*. Why? Because we have a mandate from Jesus to reach the world and what we are doing now *is not working!* It hasn't worked in years! We cannot satisfy Jesus' mandate by continuing the practices of the last fifty years! Anderson Writes,

> Changes in the community and culture must be identified and addressed if ongoing sociological renewal is to take place. A problem arises when leadership becomes entrenched in yesterday's social structures and practices.[6]

The church is an endangered species that must adapt or die. Our spiritual family is largely dysfunctional. We have a word for anything not functioning in its world: *obsolete*. The destiny of the obsolete? *Extinction!*

What is the church doing with all this? In a state of blind denial, we gather in our buildings, sing our ancient music, pray our time-worn prayers, listen to irrelevant preaching. We polish our halos and wonder why membership is dropping! Have we forgotten that our very life depends on moral

confrontation and ethical infiltration of our culture?7
This is nothing new! The methods aren't new unless
you call the work of the apostles and other disciples "new."
Simple, decisive, and substantial changes are necessary, however, to *get it out!* We either learn to get into the field of vision
and earshot of the people we seek to reach, or *lose the day!*
Posterski explains,

> What Jesus demonstrated with
> Zacchaeus is a better way. His approach
> still stands as a prototype for faithful
> and fruitful witnessing in today's soci-
> ety. He took time to be with Zacchaeus.
> He went into Zacchaeus' comfort zone.
> Instead of saying, "Come with me, there
> is a special event at my church" (Which
> is really an invitation to go where
> Christians are most comfortable), Jesus
> reversed the norm and surrendered him-
> self to the circumstances where
> Zacchaeus was most at ease.[8]

We must go where the people are and tastefully place
the gospel on the marketplace of ideas. We must meet the public on neutral ground[9] instead of requiring them to brave the
alien surroundings of our church buildings.

Relatively few churches will want to make such
changes. Sadly, most members are happy in their comfortable
ruts and wish the change agents would leave them alone.
Others *want* to change but lack the initiative or know-how.

> Yesterday's answers are not always
> appropriate for today's questions.
> Change and challenge should not be
> threatening but recognized as part of the
> process. Leaders must keep calling the

> organization and its people to the Lordship of Jesus Christ and the standards of the Bible while challenging people to grow and innovate within the biblical boundaries. Fulfilling the mission is always more important that perpetuating traditions.[10]

I talk with very few leaders among today's believers unaware that, as we now stand, we are incapable of fulfilling our mission. A basic reluctance and fearfulness regarding change paralyze action. Most leaders do not know what to do. So, they do nothing. Others, content with cosmetic changes, congratulate themselves for being *avant garde*. That's why we need to listen to Howard's story.

Sweet Surrender

Howard was going back to visit the little congregation in New Hampshire that held his heart. Fifteen years ago, fresh out of preaching school, he and Margaret joined Bob and Rose, moved to the Northeast, and established a congregation. Those early years saw outstanding success. They broadcast the gospel with all their might and God gave the increase. In five years, ten members grew to seventy-five. When he moved back to Tennessee, he thought he left a well-established, self-sufficient congregation. Within five years of leaving, however, he realized Satan was flushing most of his hard work down the devil's toilet.

Several leaders moved away. The members left behind lost their focus. When a Diotrophes[11] moved in and tried to take over, Satan hoped this deathblow would finish off the little church. When he saw trouble looming on the horizon, Howard wanted to move back. Shortly after moving back to

Tennessee, however, family needs and unavoidable circumstances required his full attention and blocked his return to New Hampshire.

One crisis seemed to follow another until ten years had come and gone. Howard could only watch. His tears, prayers, and inward agony seemed to make no difference. But now, the horizon had cleared and he could at least *try* to help the little church in some way.

Tragically, the few members that clung together were now fighting among themselves. If something didn't change very soon, only memories would remain of the work to which he gave so much. He called some of his loved ones in the little church asking if they wanted him to come and try to help. Eagerly they accepted his offer and soon he planned a three week visit.

A few weeks before the trip, reality set in. "What makes me think *I* can do anything?" "Who am I?" he thought. The closer he came to leaving, the less confident he felt. He realized that he had no magic tricks, no plan...nothing! But, he knew how to *pray.* So, pray he did. He asked the church where he preached to pray. He prayed with his wife; he prayed with the church staff. He prayed alone. One evening, a few days before he left, he and the elders knelt in the floor of his study, joined hands, and prayed for God's wisdom and blessing. As the plane took off, he prayed. As the plane landed, he was still praying.

Three weeks later, as he boarded the airliner for home, he realized an amazing transformation was taking place. He was conscious of being a catalyst to bring about change. He asked himself, "What did I *do?*" He knew he had visited, encouraged, preached, taught...just like the old days. He had urged them to stop being so inwardly occupied and return to reaching out to their community. One thing he was sure of...he had done nothing extraordinary. Two weeks after returning home, one of the New Hampshire group called. Dismayed, Howard realized the caller was crying! "Oh no!" He thought, "the whole thing has crumbled in spite of our best efforts."

"What's wrong?" asked Howard.

"Oh, nothings *wrong*," his friend said, "these are tears of *joy!* We just had our worship together, and the new spirit of love and unity is *unbelievable!* We've decided to make a genuine effort to communicate the gospel to our town."

With tear-filled eyes Howard struggled to say, "That's wonderful...just *wonderful!*"

"What a tremendous job you did here, brother," his friend said. "You really made a difference."

As he replaced the telephone in the cradle, Howard had one of those "watershed experiences" that would change his life and ministry forever. He realized that *he still did not know what he did and why it worked!* Then the dawning came: God simply answered his prayers for wisdom and discernment. But most of all, *God used him!* A greater joy than he had ever experienced filled his heart. Now he knew that change agents consist simply of surrendered and prayerful men and women who say, "Here I am, send me."

How Change Occurs

The first step to becoming a change agent is realizing that we cannot *make change happen!* While we can preach, teach, equip, challenge, encourage, and cheer people on, we cannot *force* them to change. Change comes from the *inside*, a matter of transformed minds.[12] Howard surrendered himself as a living sacrifice, God did the rest.

God working *in* us and *on* us is crucial in becoming change agents.[13] This transforming power takes us with nothing to offer and turns us into tools for his use.

For consider your calling, brethren, that there were not many wise according to the flesh, not many mighty, not many noble; but God has chosen the foolish things of the world to shame the wise, and God has chosen the weak things of the world to shame the things which are strong, and the base things of the world and the despised, God has chosen, the things that are not, that He might nullify the things that are, that no man should boast before God.[14]

All God asks of us is everything. He demands that we honor the covenant we entered as he purchased us with his son's blood. That means submissive, faith-filled renunciation of all claims to ourselves. And then, one amazing day, we realize that we *are* God's fellow-workers.[15] He can now transform us into a force to be reckoned with.

A word of caution: we can easily slip into an illusion that we carry the whole burden of change. We are but *channels* through which God brings change. The powerful Holy Spirit of God does the changing. Being the *kind of channel* that God *can* and *will* use is important. The Spirit is the electricity; we are the conductor. Glass, rubber, plastic, etc., will not conduct electricity. Indeed, as insulators they contain and limit the current. It takes *metal* to conduct electrons to light bulbs, motors, TV's, etc. *We must be made of proper stuff* before God sends his power surging through us.

I don't have to know *why* or *how* copper is a good conductor of electricity; I just need to know that it *is!* I don't have to know *why* or *how* God uses surrendered, faithful, prayerful people to change things; I just need to know that he *does!* God is able to *change* us from insulators to conductors of transforming power to ignite the fires of sacrifice. If I expect to bring others to sacrificial service, I must first lay my own body, mind, and spirit on the altar of living sacrifice.[16]

Our Lord Jesus used this mode of operation as he walked among us. He remains the peerless change agent of all time; and yet, he continually spoke of his ministry as totally surrendered to the wishes of the Father.[17] When confronted with the reality of imminent death, he had the ultimate submission to say, "Yet, not my will, but your will be done."[18] Observe his surrender! Listen to him pray!

With no resources save a bag of donated money and an occasional borrowed donkey or boat, Jesus fulfilled his purpose. He knew why he was here and what he had to do. His entire mission was to seek and save the lost, thus glorifying the Father.[19] He remained aloof from the distractions of side-issues or false alarms. He had the human race to save and he gave himself wholeheartedly to that task.

Our God is a God of change. The history of this world and God's intervention in it shouts the inescapable message: *God wants change.* His every act—sending Noah to preach to those before the flood, the promises to the patriarchs, the messages of the prophets, the sending of Jesus—generates change. In God's universe, everything moves, changes. The atoms in the most solid, stationary object contain unimaginable motion.

In history, Noah becomes a farmer, preacher, boat-builder, sailor and farmer again. Abraham, citizen of Ur, becomes a wandering nomad. The nomadic offspring of Jacob settle in Goshen, become slaves, then wandering tribes and, finally, landed gentry. Jesus, a carpenter for eighteen years, abruptly *changed* course for the cross. The church began Jewish but *changed* to accommodate the Gentiles. When early distribution methods overlooked the Grecian widows, *change* met their needs through the first deacons.[20] When Paul and Barnabas couldn't agree, they *reorganized* in order to continue.[21] We could multiply examples of change, adjustment and accommodation, to make the obvious point: Change, a vital sign of life, glorifies God and advances the cause of Christ.

On the other hand, his modern-day followers appear bent on trashing the course. Struggling through the clutter of politics and social issues, we get tangled in the rubbish of philosophical debates leading us deeper and deeper into disgusting heaps of unfocused and confusing garbage. We have forgotten that the gospel contains clean, simple solutions, no matter what the questions.

If ever we needed agents of change, we need them now. So how do we accomplish these desperately needed changes? Unless we *begin,* we never will! So...

Take the Initiative

We cannot wait for *others* to change. Unless someone gets into the starting gate, the race can't begin. If we believe that change is urgently crucial, then we must *act* as if we do. We cannot expect others to follow our lead if we never *start.* Billions wait to hear the only message that can save them. No more procrastination! If you have the courage to say, "Here I am, send me," then be prepared to *go!* If you are waiting on the Holy Spirit, you're backing up! Power and providence are already available. The sword of the Spirit is in your hand. You have a full suit of armor ready to put on (one size fits all) and weapons of righteousness for the right hand and the left.[22]

The enemy fills the horizon, ready to charge the battlefield. This is no time for another "worship service" or personal work class; now is the time to *start swinging that sword!* Storms of criticism and castigation lie ahead because some always confuse *change* with *unorthodoxy.* We must steer into the high winds and heavy seas of repudiation and disdain. No one ever won a great cause without cost. We must readily pay it.

Don't point to the other sleeping soldiers and ask, "Hey, what about them?" This is not about *them*; this is about *us!* If we keep waiting on others, we will never confront our culture with the light that exposes their deeds as evil.[23] No shouting crowds carrying placards, blocking entrances and frustrating the police, but quiet illumination of life's darkened corners.

The ways of letting our light shine before human beings are varied and limited only by our imagination. Thus, our failure to do much of *anything* is amazing. Our immobility is certainly not because we lack of *choices*. With so many exciting streets and avenues of change to choose from, it's hard to know which one to cruise down first!

Imagine a world in which we bring the gospel to our friends, associates and neighbors without the slightest hesitation and saturate our community with Christian influence. We widen our circle of acquaintances to give the gospel broad exposure. We let the happiness and joy of abundant life be seen by those stuck in the mud of misery. If we wait for a plan or a program, we will be waiting this time next year. If we wait until everyone is ready to go with us, we'll never go. Joyful people, eagerly fulfilling their purpose as lights in the world, fill the happiest churches. Visible enthusiasm is contagious!

No one can replace the people of God. Our task is neither given to, expected from, nor even possible for another people. The game is afoot; God has tagged us "it," until Jesus calls us home. God, in his loving patience, gives us time (so far) to reach his creation with his final message of rescue. Change will occur when God's people start *acting* like God's people.

Don't Major In Minors

The temptation to get bogged down in peripheral matters lies in wait, ready to waylay us. We will fail if Satan successfully distracts us from working for change that really matters! Perhaps, for example, we have concluded that the early church used fermented wine in the Lord's Supper. It would be easy enough to get in endless debates with those who disagree; but to what avail? Does it really matter? If we resolve the question one way or another, will we save more souls? Will worship become more meaningful? Edifying? Such fruitless debates invite Satan to devour the debaters. We must carefully choose our battles.

The same thing is true for cosmetic changes. We all know people whose face is a work of art. Catch them without their paint and the difference can be startling. Cosmetic changes in the church consist primarily of changes in worship assemblies. Introductions of drama, contemporary songs, more non-traditional involvement of those assembled, though perhaps beneficial, all qualify as cosmetics. In spite of our over-emphasis on the Sunday worship assembly, these are surface considerations and therefore secondary considerations. Really, we need to...

Keep A Clear View of Priorities

Most Christians and churches I know are really skilled at the fine art of getting carts before the horses. For example, some bemoan stiff and lifeless worship assemblies, unenthusiastic singing, drearily predictable communion services, and repetitious, impersonal prayers. "We need more celebration!" we cry. "Give us exciting, meaningful, and edifying worship experiences!" But apathetic worship services reflect apathetic hearts. Even among groups where exuberant worship rules, it often becomes form without substance. Dr. Mark Hanby, of the Charismatic persuasion, writes:

> We have lost our wholeness and moved into "production religion," where we must produce a certain line of preachers or singers, or the people won't be moved. That's because they've been trained to desire talent, not the Spirit. God is weary of our carnality.
>
> We tolerate the move of the Holy Spirit until the clock on the back wall says it's time to dismiss and go home — then we promptly close our Bibles and put the Holy Spirit back in the box like a trained rabbit. When the appointed day comes around again, religion says its time to go back and do it again.[24]

Times of worship for Christians consciously and consistently living for Jesus and seeking and saving the lost, are *automatically* joyful and enthusiastic. We can successfully create *artificial exuberance.* Our priority ought to be changing unfocused, distracted church-attenders into true disciples of Christ who rejoice *naturally.*

Get On Your Knees

A formidable obstacle to change agents is loneliness. When others don't feel the same strong sense of mission and commitment, discouragement comes easily. Discouragement remains the devil's chief instrument for crippling Christians into inactivity. If you feel as if you are struggling all alone, remember that there are many like you out there. They are probably fighting discouragement also. Look for them and, if you find them, pray, work, and study together. Together you can be a major force in bringing about changes that result in God's glory.

There is power in immediate, fervent prayer, and perhaps, fasting. Get down on your knees with others who share your convictions and pour your hearts out to God. His Spirit will provide comfort and renewed strength to go on alone, if necessary. We are *all* going to have to get on our knees if we expect to get the church back on its feet!

God has consistently said, "Yes" to our prayers for contact with hearts open and hungry for the gospel. Pray fervently and regularly that he will use you and your fellow-warriors to bring about the changes that must come. Then, simply make yourselves available. Be sensitive to his answer.

Be Willing To Risk

The forefathers of America risked everything, including their lives, for the sake of liberty. Can you think of anything worthwhile ever accomplished without risk? Each step in the march of advancing civilization involves risky business. Cowards never began a revolution. Wishy-washy porridge-like faith ventures nothing and gains nothing. If you and I want to bring about a revolution, we must leave the relative safety of our homes. We must forsake the dulling comfort of air-conditioned and cushioned church buildings and test the mettle of our faith. C.S. Lewis wrote,

> You never know how much you really believe anything until its truth or falsehood becomes a matter of life and death to you. It is easy to say you believe a rope to be strong and sound as long as you are merely using it to cord a box. But suppose you had to hang by that

rope over a precipice. Wouldn't you then first discover how much you really trusted it? Only a real risk tests the reality of a belief.[25]

We must risk homes, lives, and sacred fortunes. We must risk ostracism and ridicule...even from those among our own fellowships.

What made the reformers reformers? They were ordinary people, ready to risk things we humans hold most precious, for truth and righteousness. They risked everything to decry the abuse, scandal, corruption, and outright error characterizing the church of their time.

A distinction of those who make major changes in their world is a willingness to risk all for their cause. Such heroes spurn old lovers such as Comfort, Acceptance, and Prosperity to embrace *Truth* and *Righteousness*.

Does Jesus expect less of me than *he* gave? He left heaven's indescribable joy and beauty; we must deny ourselves the *world* to reach it.

He willingly left the comforts of home and hearth. We willingly leave these behind for a home, eternal in the heavens.

He consented to suffer the indignities heaped upon him by those in power; we also agree to suffering before glorification.

He gave his life to the total exploitation of the Father; we give ourselves in sweet submission.

Jesus is coming again. He came the first time as God and human blended in the form of a Jewish Carpenter from Nazareth. He taught, performed miracles, fulfilled prophecies—all for the purpose of producing faith.[26] Faith both demands and offers. It demands our commitment to draw trust from the well of belief. It offers power beyond human comprehension.

Now, nearly two millennia later, his followers have the opportunity to answer the most serious and searching question he ever asked: *"When the Son of Man comes, will He find faith on the earth?"*[27]

[1]John Naisbitt, *Megatrends,* Warner Books, Inc. 75 Rockefeller Plaza, New York, N.Y. 10019, 1982, pp. 85,86

[2]Leith Anderson, *Dying For Change,* Bethany House Publishers, Minneapolis, Minnesota, 55438, 1990, p.136.

[3] John Naisbitt, pp 88,94.

[4]Donald C. Posterski, *Reinventing Evangelism,* Intervarsity Press, Downers Grove, Illinois, U.S.A., 1989, p. 65

[5]I.e., she liked my sermons.

[6]Leith Anderson, Op.Cit., p. 130

[7]Ephesians 5:3ff; I Corinthians 5:9,10; Philippians 2:15

[8]Donald C. Posterski, Op.Cit., p. 29

[9] Homes were frequently used in the first century. It is still the best place today!

[10]Leith Anderson, Op.cit., p. 136.

[11]3 John 9ff

[12]Romans 12:2

[13]Philippians 2:12,13

[14]I Corinthians 1:26-29 (NASB)

[15]I Corinthians 3:9

[16]Romans 12:1,2

[17]John 5:30; 6:38

[18]Mark 14:36

[19]Luke 19:10

[20]Acts 6:1-7

[21]Acts 15:36-41

[22]Ephesisans 6:10ff; 2 Cor. 6:6,7

[23]Ephesians 5:6-13

[24]Dr. Mark Hanby, "God's Lambing Grounds," *Destiny Image Digest*, July/August 1993, pp 10,11.

[25]C.S. Lewis, *A Grief Observed*, p. 25, from *The Quotable Lewis*, Wayne Martindale and Jerry Root, editors, Tyndale House Publishers, Inc., Wheaton Illinois, 1989, p.66.

[26]John 20:30,31

[27] Luke 18:8 (NASB)

FOR REFLECTION & STUDY

1. The Church in Chains

1. What process has allowed the cause of Christ to be confined?
2. In what ways has our civilization suffered from our
   confinement?
3. Read Romans 10 and discuss how it personally applies to
   you.
4. Read again the definition of RADICAL on page 10.
   What changes would have to take place for *you* to become
   a radical Christian?

2. In the Footsteps of our Leader

1. What is your personal image of the Christ?
2. What is the significance of our designation as "the body of
   Christ?"
   How can we display his magnificence, love, and glory to
   our world?
   What has caused our emphases to be so different from
   that of Jesus and the apostles? Make a list.
3. Describe either a humorous or serious time when a manual
   or a map made your life simpler.
4. What are some of the chief hindrances to restarting Jesus'
   revolution?
   What are some evidences of misplaced emphases?
   What will a revitalized revolution require of you person-
   aly?

3. The New Testament Way

1. What are some ways the church can overcome the "fortress
   mentality?"

2. Read Hebrews 10:25 in context.
   Considering the purposes of assembly, what can individual Christians do to make sure those purposes are fulfilled?
3. Following Christ means taking action. What gift or gifts do you have that could be put into action for the cause of Christ? Share these with your group.
4. What are some things that personally hinder you from active discipleship?

4. Gaining Credibility

1. Define "credibility."
   Why do we need it as Christians?
   What can individual Christians do to give credibility to the gospel?
2. How should the church envision itself and what impact should that make upon our use of time, talent, and money?
3. What are some results of our indoor, invisible brand of Christianity?
   What steps would be necessary to make our practice of Christianity more visible?
4. Why does the church have little or no impact on our culture — even in areas where we are numerically strong?
5. In what ways does denominationalism hinder the cause of Christ?
   What can be done about it?

5. Words You Can Eat

1. Describe a positive or negative personal experience that taught you the power of words?
2. Read Proverbs 25:11; 1CO 14:26; EPH 4:29. What does the Holy Spirit teach is the chief purpose of our speech to one another?
3. Describe an experience, either personal or observed, that demonstrated to you the importance of tact.
4. Discuss what is necessary for productive dialogue between

people or groups that disagree.

6. What a Message!

1. Read what Paul said about relating to people of different backgrounds and circumstances (1 Corinthians 9:19-22). How do we apply this to the way we personally spread the gospel?
2. In what ways has the gospel brought light to your relationships at home, work or school?
3. List three ways the Way has brought blessings to you or your family.
4. Re-read Acts 4:18-20. Why do you think Peter and John could not keep silent?
   What is wrong when we are able to remain silent or otherwise inactive?

7. War

1. Have you known or observed true soldiers of Christ? Describe their actions.
   What are some possible reasons our soldiers are not ready for battle?
2. Read Ephesians 5:3-14. What can children of light do to dispel the darkness in our communities? Be specific and practical.
3. What are the goals of Satan? Make a list.
   Has he been successful?
4. Give some examples of how you or your church have take both defensive and offensive action against the forces of darkness.
5. Re-read "Diotrephes and His Kin" (pages 84-86). Tell about a "Diotrephes" you have encountered.
   How did he work?
   What was the outcome?

6. Read Romans 8:37; James 4:7; 1 John 4:4 and Romans 16:20 in their contexts.
   What are the promises?
   What are the conditions?

8. Monkey Wrenches

1. Why does the church in so many places offer little or no threat to Satan?
2. In scripture, pastors, elders, and bishops are different descriptions for the same persons (Acts 20:17 "elders"; 20:28 "overseer" = bishop; "shepherd" = pastor). Why are godly, visionary pastors so important to the church?
3. Discuss rules and traditions.
   What must always be their source?
   How can custom get in the way of progress?
   How can we deal with these hindrances?
4. Review pages 99-100. How have we, as rank and file members, contributed to the rise of professionalism? What changes can we make to correct the problem?

9. Natural Evangelism

1. What do all outreach programs and methods have in common?
   What does this mean to you as an individual disciple?
2. What attracts people to busy, growing churches?
   Discuss the pro's and con's of such growth.
3. Take a poll of Christians you know (or those in your group).
   How many were brought to Christ through assemblies?
   Campaigns?
   Public Preaching?
   Another person?
4. Read 1 Corinthians 3:5-9. Have you ever been instrumental in bringing a soul to Christ?
   Are you active in planting or watering? How?

5. Make a list of family, friends, and neighbors you want to share the gospel with.
   Pray along with your group for opportunities to do this.
   Pray for the wisdom to see God's answers.

10. The Dreaming

1. Read Ephesians 3:20; 2 Corinthians 6:7; and 2 Corinthians 9:8-11.
   What do you dream for your congregation?
   What do you dream for your personal ministry?
   Are these impossible dreams? Why?
2. How should we respond to those who say things like:
   We can't afford it.
   We tried that once.
   We've never tried that.
   Think where it might lead! ?
3. List some reasons why the church is sleepy, saints are comfortable and unaware of Satan's activity.
4. By what process do our dreams come true?

11. Let's Get Practical

1. Why do you think churches have difficulty taking the direction Jesus originally intended?
   Discuss what can be done to get back on track.
2. Read over the "Ten Practical Steps to Revolution" beginning on page 139. Now, write down the numbers 1-10. Put a plus (+) beside the steps you are already taking and a minus (-) beside those you need to take. Share these with your group and pray for God's help to take them.
3. Read over the proposal beginning on page 141.
   What proposals would you make regarding your church?
   Discuss each proposal and the purpose for it.
4. Read 1 Peter 3:15. What should be our reaction to people who question us about our faith and hope?

12. Revolutionary Prayer

1. Take inventory of your prayer practices. Are you satisfied? If not, what needs to change? How?
2. Re-read the section on "Labor" beginning on page 154. Think of a time when prayer was the last thing you wanted to do. Share this with your group.
3. Rethink the importance of prayer to the first disciples. As a church, how do our practices differ from theirs?
4. Discuss the link between revolution and prayer. Discuss why prayer is essential.

13. The Change Agents

1. Discuss the relevance of your church to the conditions and needs of your community.
   Do empty pews testify to irrelevance?
   Is your church winning souls or collecting the saved from other places?
   What changes need to occur to become relevant to your community?
   If you are part of a church experiencing true growth (conversions), what changes were made to become relevant?
2. Re-read the story of Howard.
   What were the chief characteristics that enabled him to bring about change?
3. Think about the changes needed in your church. List the main obstacles to achieving them.
4. Think about issues that have divided believers through history. Make a list.
   Which ones have been over insignificant, surface opinions?
   Which ones have been important enough to become tests of fellowship?

ORDER FORM

Postal orders:
> Somerset Road Press
> 381 Casa Linda Plaza, #229
> Dallas, TX 75218

Please send me __(s) copies of *The Urgent Revolution*.

Name _____

Address_____

City_____State_____Zip_____

Telephone (___)_____

Sales Tax
Please add 6.25% for books shipped to Texas addresses.

Shipping
Book Rate: $2.00 for the first book and 75 cents for each additional book (Surface shipping may take three to four weeks)
Air Mail: $3.50 per book

*Please send check or money order only.

On-Line inquiries:
> somersetroad@safeweb.net

Thank you